The Simple Plan

Six Easy Steps to Make Millions from Your Ideas

Ken Johnson

The Simple Plan

The Simple Plan

Six Easy Steps to Make Millions from Your Ideas

by Kenneth R. Johnson

Published by

Grand Legacy Corporation

30110 Orchard Lake Road, Farmington Hills, Michigan 40334

mailto:kenjohn1@att.net

Grand Legacy Corporation

What others are saying about...

The Simple Plan

Six Easy Steps to Make Millions from Your Ideas

"Ken Johnson is the most awesome inventor and it's a pleasure to have known him all these years. He invented what is most people's favorite card game, Phase 10. It is still currently selling in stores all over the USA. When Ken is invited to speak somewhere, he packs the house and sells out. He & I teamed up to work together and spoke at the Chicago Houseware Show which also had a great turnout. Ken's book will help inventors and I know it will be really successful because he has a lot of valuable information & resources to offer to inventors. I wish you much more success, Ken!"

- Joe Finkler, Grand Rapids Inventors Network

****

"I have had the pleasure of knowing and working with Ken Johnson for over six years. As the President of the Jackson Inventors Network (JIN), and the Chairman of the Michigan Inventor's Coalition (MIC), I have been exposed to the majority of inventors in the state. MIC is a group that supports and represents all of the inventor groups in the greater Michigan area. These groups have grown and have the reputation of providing greater success for inventors. As per the U.S. Patent Office, Michigan Inventor's Coalition has made Michigan the #1 inventor support state in the country. This has been done from the effort of many caring and hard-working inventors helping inventors. Ken Johnson is one of them.

"Ken is one of the most successful inventors in the state of Michigan. He has been a presenter for my Jackson Group, The Detroit Area Inventors Group, Muskegon, and the Grand Rapids Inventors groups, but most importantly, Ken has been a presenter and Board Member of the Michigan Inventor's Coalition. His guidance, direction, and inspiration have provided the information and needed help to move numerous inventors past the idea stage to the market stage or the licensing stage. Ken's experience and knowledge is unmatchable. We (creative inventors and entrepreneurs) consider him one of the best assets in the state of Michigan as an inventor, entrepreneur, and an investor in new products and ideas.

"Ken has now put together a book, sharing his first innovations, his experiences in the process, his insight, advice, knowledge, mistakes not to make, and shortcuts to succeeding in projects. Ken Johnson is successful in what he has done and has used this experience and skills to help guide others to succeed. I personally feel blessed to have his help with Michigan inventors. Ken's book is a must-have."

- John D. Hopkins, Chairman, Michigan Inventors Coalition; President,

Jackson Inventors Network

****

"I have known Ken Johnson for about 10 years. The inventive success of Ken's game Phase 10 and my game Sequence has cemented our common desire to see the best games possible being available for public play and enjoyment. Our friendship goes beyond being fellow inventors. We have developed a sincere and respectful friendship – a kinship – because we have both lived through the highs and lows of the inventing process, not to mention the ups and downs of licensing our inventions.

"I believe *The Simple Plan* will prove to be THE textbook for aspiring game inventors. Ken has covered virtually every aspect of inventing and selling a new game. You'll learn everything, from your original idea to seeing your idea on the market – and everything in between.

"While success can never be guaranteed, following a tried-and-true, step-by-step blueprint, developed over decades of sweat and tears – experiencing both great success and deep disappointing failure – will greatly enhance the inventor's chance of seeing their invention on a store shelf. And trust me, there is NOTHING like seeing your invention on a store shelf – well, maybe seeing it in someone's shopping cart might be better."

- Doug Reuter, Inventor of the Sequence game

******

"Ken Johnson's book, *The Simple Plan*, is a valuable source of information for every entrepreneur. This three-part book covers the Inventor Mindset, The Simple Plan, and Intellectual Property. In the Inventor Mindset, Johnson tells his story of product development as a young adult, working from the basement of his family home. He shares worthwhile lessons learned from challenges of innovation, marketing, manufacturing, and licensing his now successful Phase 10 card game. Decades of experience in product development give Johnson extensive knowledge of how an inventor can avoid common mistakes and maintain a positive mindset.

"Part Two of the book outlines six steps for successful product development: research, prototype, evaluation, provisional patent application, intellectual property registration, and decision on whether to license or manufacture your product. Johnson emphasizes the order of the steps as well as the importance of timing. Finally, Patents, Copyrights, and Trademarks are introduced in the last section of the book.

"As a board member of the Inventor's Association of Metropolitan Detroit (IAMD) since 2011, I have had the pleasure of hearing Ken Johnson speak on numerous occasions. He is an excellent and effective speaker who has served on the board of this organization for years. Johnson has spoken to IAMD on many occasions, as well as serving as a classroom guest speaker in university entrepreneurship courses, and as a keynote speaker at the Michigan Inventor's Coalition annual EXPO conference.

"Ken Johnson has been a patient and encouraging mentor to countless Michigan entrepreneurs. Now, as an author of *The Simple Plan,* his prized knowledge can be shared with a wider audience. Johnson's book will be an invaluable addition to any entrepreneur's library!"

- Catherine Phillips, Librarian, Lawrence Technological University; and Board of Directors, Inventor's Association of Metro Detroit.

****

"I have had the privilege of interacting with Ken Johnson for over three years. During that time, Ken's expertise and success as both an inventor and a businessman have made me eager to ask for more and seek his industry expertise. His knowledge of both venturing and licensing product is both simple and detailed. Ken has been in the industry for over 30 years and brings a portfolio of experience, advice, and honest direction for any new inventor. He is able to articulate the "do's and don'ts" that are most commonly asked in this industry based on his successes and failures. His experience with inventor groups, USPTO, and licensing to companies provides an abundance of resources for any new inventor, yet does so in a way that provides a clear path to success.

"As an inventor and entrepreneur, I followed the venturing path with my product, Thegreenglovedryer (now revised generation 2, TheEcoDryer). As Ken highlights in his book, venturing is not for every entrepreneur as it requires advanced business acumen skills and experience to navigate.

"After years of speaking to new entrepreneurs and inventors, I have consistently said, 'If I had to do it over, I would have chosen the licensing route.' Ken's six steps in this book will provide any inventor a clear path to increased success, as well as the potential financial income desired by accurately negotiating licensing deals, and provide the freedom and time to continue to create and innovate."

- Karen Smoots, Inventor and Entrepreneur, TheEcoDryer by Thegreenglovedryer

DEDICATION

To all people with an inventive spirit – Acting on it can transform your life and possibly that of the world of humankind.

&

To my wife Valerie and son Christian

&

To my father William and mother Margarette, who were a source of encouragement and help during my early days inventing.

Acknowledgments

I am grateful to many people:

Valerie and Christian for providing the inspiration that drives me every day.

Ken Wachsberger for editing and cheerleading this effort from day one. Without your prodding this book might not have ever been finished. You are an awesome editor and writer and a source of encouragement for every writer and would-be writer who has crossed your path.

Joe Finkler, John D. Hopkins, Doug Reuter, Catherine Phillips, Karen Smoots, David Fedewa, Ken Yee, and Joseph Shields for your encouragement and for writing reviews. Without your encouragement I may not have written this book.

Karen Bonnici for your support and feedback after a time-consuming reread of the entire manuscript. You are an excellent and creative inventor. I know your invention Super Blanky® and other products will continue to do well.

Joe and Hannah Finkler, Joseph Shields, Jerome Feig, Catherine Phillips, Mary Kordyban, Ken Yee, and Ken and Emily Wachsberger for helping me pick a cool cover design.

Cal Sharp for cover design and internal page layout. Awesome work!

Meghan McGowan for indexing this book. You said this was the first book you've indexed. Great job!

The inventor community, including members of the Inventor Association of Metro Detroit (IAMD) and the Michigan Inventors Coalition (MIC). I've spoken at many such groups all over the country and have been most excited and encouraged by your inventive spirit. This book is for you!

Table of Contents

Foreword

The first time I met Ken Johnson was at a gathering of inventors in Michigan where he was the keynote speaker. I had heard about him and his remarkable accomplishments, so I was surprised to discover that he was so down to earth and willing to give so much good advice. In fact, he stayed the whole day.

Most experts are not willing to give up their blueprint for success. They hold back a bit, sometimes a lot.

In the past decade, I've visited many inventor groups. Typically, speakers at these events focus on one or two aspects of the process of bringing a product to market. Very seldom do you meet someone who has experienced all of it — and thus is able to talk about what's really required to take a sketch on a napkin to commercialization and market success. Speaking from experience, this is no easy feat. These are the people inventors need to learn from, because their insights are genuinely priceless.

Typically, these people are extremely busy!

What was truly amazing about Ken? He had nothing to sell. He was giving back and giving it all up.

When it comes to inventing, you need to be extremely careful about the advice you take to heart. Many people are just trying to sell you their services. They haven't put in the work. They haven't obtained the knowledge they're sharing through determination and persistence, resulting in a lifetime of achievement.

Ken Johnson is truly an expert. When I consider that his game Phase 10 has been selling for more than 35 years, my head nearly explodes. It continues to be one of the most popular games in the world! *Wow*.

I'll never forget watching him share his precious advice and being so patient with so many inventors that day in Michigan.

Thankfully for all of us, he's decided to give back even more with his new book, The Simple Plan. In it, he outlines six simple steps anyone can follow to achieve licensing success regardless of what category they're inventing in.

Most books that I've read about inventing overcomplicate this process. Not Ken. He takes the reader behind the scenes and breaks down each step
into bite-size pieces, showing us just how doable licensing is.

After licensing my own ideas for products, I began educating inventors more than 20 years ago. Ken's advice is spot on — and hard won.

There's nothing like seeing something you invented on a store shelf. It's
magic. I'll forever treasure the memory of watching a commercial for the
Michael Jordan-Wall Ball — the most successful toy I invented and licensed
— with my family on a Saturday morning.

The toy industry is a wonderful place. These companies need your ideas. But, like anything else, to become successful you need good information. Ken supplies it to you in this book

Ken, I cannot thank you enough for being an ambassador to the inventing
community. Your dedication and commitment are incredible.

— Stephen Key, award-winning inventor and inventRight cofounder.

Introduction

Thank you for purchasing this book. I wrote it to help you navigate the process of bringing your new invention idea to market.

I've spent years developing and understanding and honing this process. I've experienced failure and I've had success. I'm grateful for the failure side because I've learned a great deal from it. It led me to the success side. Today you can go into stores all over the world and see my products. You can go online and see my products. They generate millions of hits on Google, in particular Phase 10, my most successful, which is now being distributed by Mattel.

Other games I've created have had success for periods of time. They include

- Dice Baseball
- Caught-Cha card game
- Converge
- Monarch
- Word Master
- Bible Pocket Trivia
- Assumption
- GABU – Galactic Bugs
- Phase 10 Masters Edition
- Phase 10 Dice
- Phase 10 Twist
- Phase 10 Kids
- Phase 10 MOD
- Phase 10 for Mobile Devices
- Electronic Phase 10 (handheld electronic version)
- Stake Your Stash

Along the way, I founded the Inventors Academy and created *The Simple Plan: Six Easy Steps to Make Millions from Your Ideas*.

The Purpose of This Book

Teaching you *The Simple Plan* is the purpose of this book. My goal is to help you understand everything from A to Z about the inventing process and the marketing of new inventions. You will learn exactly what it takes to be successful as an inventor and what it takes to launch a successful product that will generate income for you, as a licensor, or revenue, as a business owner manufacturing your invention. You will discover ways to avoid pitfalls and you will find shortcuts to the top of the steep learning curve that is involved in the inventing process.

I created my six-step plan after years of trial and error. I also studied a lot about the inventing process and ways to use the elements of that process to launch my own inventions. What I found interesting as a young inventor was the fact that there was no one resource or place where I could go to get good information.

Even today, there are a lot of good books you can buy on Amazon. Many are written by successful inventors. You can find many websites that claim to provide help for inventors. Even the United States Patent & Trademark Office (USPTO) offers some insight and information to inventors.

However, what I found lacking back then as a young, new inventor that is still true today was this: NONE of the information I could find was comprehensive enough. Most would only give me an overview of what I needed to do. NONE drilled down to the exact steps necessary for inventing success.

Even more frustrating for today's new inventor is the fact that some of the books and websites make the inventing process seem more complex than it really is. After reviewing many of the books in the marketplace today and viewing the websites dedicated to helping inventors, coupled with my knowledge of the inventing process, I decided to write this book.

My simple plan provides the answer. It is a synthesis of my trial-and-error experiences and the information that I learned from others.

You see, I have found the process of creating and launching a successful invention to be really quite simple. Yes, it's simple. It's not complicated. While each step has its challenges, none of the steps are difficult. You just need to know what the steps are.

The Simple Plan tells you. It is a step-by-step guide, with insight on issues that will concern you along the way and specific instructions on what you need to *do* and in what order it must be done.

Timing Matters

Why is this important? Because, as I discovered when I was just starting out, in the inventing process, timing matters.

- *You don't* do the analysis or the evaluation after you apply for a patent, in most cases.

- *You don't* build a prototype before you've done an initial research evaluation, in most cases.

- *And you certainly don't* try to get a license agreement before you've done a proper research evaluation or developed a prototype, in most cases.

I say "in most cases" because there may be exceptions. But for the most part, for 99% of you, you will follow the six steps – that's all there are – that I outline in *The Simple Plan* in their precise order. If you follow this outline, and if you complete the steps properly, you will magnify your chance of success.

Now, some books out there detail all kinds of processes inventors could or should do. They may tell you, "You need to do an evaluation." Or, "There are 150 different ways to make a prototype. You need to make one. Here's how." Or they'll tell you, "You need to get a license agreement for your baby product. Find the names of ten baby product manufacturers that make products similar to what you've created, send each a letter, and tell them you've got this great idea." However, most don't tell you *when* to implement these steps.

Order Matters

While that may be a valid approach, my plan delivers more detail to you in the proper order and with the proper perspective on how and when things should be done. I have found that by keeping it simple, most of my students and clients have had greater opportunity for success. The steps are clear. I detail them specifically. If you learn them and do them correctly, you can be successful with your invention.

When I started out as an inventor over forty years ago, I didn't find any books on the subject. There were probably a few out there, but they certainly weren't as readily available as they are today. There was no Internet. There was no Amazon. There were libraries, of course, but the books I found back then were generally technical or vague about the steps an inventor should take. Then, as now, most books will tell you "what to do" but not "when" or "in what order" to do the steps.

Only through persistence, continued research, trial and error, and by spending money going down what turned out to be many dead ends was I able to determine the proper path to success. I discovered that if I took this path *every time* my chances for success were greatly increased. When I veered onto a wrong path, failure was most likely to result.

Many of you have been "inventing" for some period of time. You may have several ideas or products you've been conceptualizing and developing. No doubt you have faced roadblocks throughout the process. *The Simple Plan* will give you the understanding you need to successfully bring your invention ideas to the marketplace.

You will learn how the process works, why it's worked for me and others, and how to make your invention the success that you know it can be.

In separate chapters, I discuss the six steps that make up *The Simple Plan:*

1. Research Evaluation
2. Prototype Development
3. Product Evaluation
4. Provisional Patent Application
5. Intellectual Property Registration
6. License/Venture

These are the six steps. They're simple in that they are easy to identify. Don't get me wrong, though. It's going to require some work on your part, some effort, and some time, but most of the steps aren't that difficult. It's just a matter of getting it done.

I've watched inventors struggle, some for years. Just the other day I was at a local inventors' club. A certain gentleman was sitting behind me. He called out my name and I turned around. He asked me a question. I looked on the table in front of him and saw several jars filled with some kind of cream. I asked him what was in the jars. He said they contained a facial cream that had been invented by a woman he knew. To date, he said, she had spent about $17,000 on a patent for this cream. He shook his head. He thought she had wasted a lot of money.

You can imagine my response. I was thinking, "What a colossal waste of money!" Why do I consider her spending $17,000 for an *issued* patent a waste of money? Because she didn't evaluate the marketplace. She is still struggling to get that invention out there.

Had she done a research evaluation, step 1 of *The Simple Plan*, she would have known more clearly, before she even made the prototype for this facial cream, step 2, whether her invention had a real chance at commercial success in the marketplace. If the first two steps didn't give her a conclusive answer, she would have done the product evaluation, step 3. She would have then learned more about her commercial chances because she would have let consumers sample her product and she would have asked them:

- What do you think?
- What would you pay?

and the other appropriate questions I outline in *The Simple Plan*. After such surveying she would have known whether she had an invention worth pursuing.

She would not have spent $17,000 on a patent. Registration of a patent is step 5. You must successfully complete the first three steps before you even get to it. If you get to that fifth step on any invention and you complete it, you should have a strong chance of success because you've done all your homework. You've built a prototype; you know it works the way it is supposed to work. You have evaluated the marketplace, the competition, the patentability. You know what the competition is doing. You know what your invention will cost you to build and how it's going to be manufactured. You know what people will pay for it. You know all of this before you've applied for your patent. You will not, like my friend's friend, have wasted $17,000 on a patent that will never get you even a dime.

If you learn nothing else from this book, please, don't spend money on a patent before you've completed all the steps that come before it. In 2014, the U.S. Patent Office issued 300,000 utility patents. a good percentage of

7

which were issued to independent inventors like you. I can't tell you how frustrating it is to know that over 90% of them will not yield a dime to the inventor, let alone the cost of the patent. Why? Because the inventor ran to the patent office to apply for a patent before determining if the product would sell.

Did you know that you are not required to build a working, functioning prototype in order to apply for a patent? Do you know that you can apply for a patent before you even know whether or not the invention will work, if it will accomplish the job for which it was created, or if it will perform efficiently? It may work on paper, but does it work in reality? Too many inventors don't know because they have never built a prototype, given it to potential consumers, and said, "Try this. Let me know what you think."

If you don't follow my six simple steps, you may discover too late that your invention doesn't work, or it doesn't work well, or consumers won't pay the retail price that you are asking. You would have wasted your money on an expensive patent that you didn't need.

True, not all inventors have the resources to create a prototype. They may be limited financially. But most inventions can be prototyped for a lot less than you probably think. If you keep the idea simple, prototypes can be cobbled together from existing products or made inexpensively through 3D printing and other methods, as I'll show you later in this book. For those that can't be done without a great deal of resources, it might be better to go ahead and get a patent and then create the prototype with the help of investors and others who have a stake in it. Later in this book I'll present this approach in detail, too.

I know you're concerned about protecting your ideas. I know you're concerned about someone beating you to the patent office. However, if 300,000 patents are issued annually and most do not yield enough money even to recover the cost of the patent, it tells you that too many people are applying for patents on products that are not commercially viable. Don't be one of them. Don't waste your money. Keep it in your pocket until you know you have a product that *will sell*.

The Simple Plan is the process of evaluating and preparing your invention for the market and getting it out there in just six steps.

Preparing Your Mind

However, before you approach step 1, you must prepare yourself. You must go through the idea creation and development stage. And you must develop your personal mindset as an inventor and entrepreneur. You will learn about these pre-stages in the first few chapters of this book.

In my view *all success comes from thought.* Look around you right now. Everything you see began as a thought in someone's mind. You could be that someone if you remain positive, keep your wits about you, continue to create ideas in your mind, and then translate them into both a written and a tangible form.

Don't spin your wheels on an invention that's going nowhere!

If your idea is going nowhere, admit it and move on to a new idea. I mean, you're an inventor. You're an idea person, a creator. If one idea isn't working, formulate a new one. Find a new problem and invent a solution. There are plenty of problems that need an innovator like you.

My first game, Dice Baseball, didn't succeed in the marketplace. I could have sat back and wallowed in my misery. Or I could have kept beating that dead horse and trying to make that game a success when the market was telling me otherwise. The third option was to move on, come up with a new idea.

I took the third option. When it was clear I wouldn't succeed with Dice Baseball, I learned what I could from my failure and then let it go. I came up with Phase 10, the card game that became a bestseller around the world. I've made millions of dollars as a result of its success. I continue to earn global sales royalties. I'm grateful I didn't get emotionally attached to my first failed idea.

Don't you either. If your idea doesn't work, if the market doesn't want it, if it can't be produced at a price people will pay, if it doesn't effectively or efficiently resolve the problem, or if the problem itself that you're trying to resolve isn't great enough and doesn't have enough numbers to make any real money, then don't do it. Find another idea, resolve a different problem, and make money with that new idea or the next one or the next one.

My goal is to help you succeed as an inventor. Success as an inventor means coming up with a product that you can give to the world, that people

9

can use for enjoyment or to resolve their problems and fulfill their needs. That's one reason for being an inventor.

The second reason is to make money! You want to make money as an inventor to fulfill *your* dreams, so that you can live the lifestyle that you've dreamed of for yourself.

You want to stop punching a clock for someone else. Or you want to land a license deal that allows you to sit back and collect royalties. Both are satisfying options. I've done both. So can you.

Part 1:

The Inventor Mindset

Chapter 1

My Story

"The true sign of intelligence is not knowledge but imagination."
Albert Einstein

*"You measure the size of the accomplishment by the obstacles
you had to overcome to reach your goals."*
Booker T. Washington

I was 12-years old when I created my first invention. It was a baseball board game I called Dice Baseball. I created that game with the help of my brother and sister.

The three of us played the game together through our teenage years. It was a fun game, and it was simple. We threw four dice and counted the numbers that showed up. The possible combination of numbers was anywhere from 4, if you had 1 on each die, to 24, if you rolled all 6's. So from 4 to 24, whatever total resulted from the throw, we had a chart that interpreted what that throw meant in baseball terms.

For instance, if you threw a 17, your batter got a single. If you threw a 15, it was a strike out. After playing this game for years, we determined the odds of certain numbers coming up. The more frequently recurring numbers usually resulted in a strikeout, a ground out, a fly out, or an out of some kind. The less frequently thrown numbers resulted in singles, doubles, triples, or home runs.

This outcome more closely simulated a real baseball game because, after all, if you're batting .300, you are considered a great hitter even though you are only hitting the ball safely three out of ten tries.

As kids, 12- and 13-years old, we figured this out: that frequently thrown numbers should result in outs and less frequently thrown numbers should result in hits or advancements along the base path. We created the game to produce that outcome.

Part 1 - The Inventor Mindset

My First Invention

At the age of 19, I was working at Ford Motor Company as a welder. While I enjoyed welding, it was not the job or career I wanted to spend the rest of my life doing. Then suddenly, during a downturn in the automotive industry, I got laid off.

I figured the layoff was an opportunity for me to get into business. I wanted to do something on my own, to have a business of my own. So I started thinking, "What can I do? What business can I get into?

Then it came to me: I would start a game company and my first game would be Dice Baseball. And that's what I did.

But it wasn't easy. I didn't have any business mentors. I didn't have resources, financial or otherwise. I didn't know anybody in the industry.

I didn't really know anything about business, only that I wanted to be in it. My strong desire outstripped my lack of knowledge and resources.

I studied and I learned and I talked to enough people that eventually I figured out how to launch my game. But I made many mistakes along the way.

The first thing I thought to do was to contact one of the invention marketing companies I had seen for years in the back pages of magazines and on late-night TV. So I contacted Invention Marketing Incorporated (IMI). In fact, I still have the paperwork they sent me, the report that they provided me as a result of my enrollment in their program.

In their correspondence with me, they asked me to send a description of my game and some general information. I did as instructed and sent them what they requested along with a check for a few hundred dollars. A few weeks later, they sent me a glowing report that indicated that my game was the "greatest game that we have ever seen" and assured me that "there are millions to be made." There was so much hype in this report that, on the one hand, I thought, "This is great. I'm going to make a lot of money." It was everything an inventor could hope to hear.

On the other hand, I thought to myself – and again I was just 19 or 20 at the time – "Wait a minute; this just seems too easy." It looked as though the report was a "boilerplate" document. You could take my company and my invention name out and plug in another company and invention name and you could give this same report to someone else. It wasn't at all personalized.

At the time I had never heard of the word "boilerplate" but I knew that the report they sent me could have been sent to just about anyone. That made me suspicious.

In addition, they wanted me to send them another $2,500, on top of the few hundred dollars that I had already sent them, to provide their "services," which included introducing my game to the marketplace through a license deal. They indicated that they would approach game manufacturers on my behalf seeking a license deal with them. That was forty years ago, but the same basic approach is still used today by such companies.

So, for both of those reasons – because I was suspicious and because I didn't want to spend $2,500 – I decided not to continue with them.

But, I thought, okay, if I'm not going to work with Invention Marketing Incorporated, my next step must be to contact game manufacturing companies and publishers and attempt to get a licensing deal myself, as that's what IMI said they were going to do. Through a license deal, the licensee would manufacture and distribute my game and pay me a royalty.

So that was the next move I made. I looked in the *Thomas Register of American Manufacturers* and the Yellow Pages. I visited toy stores, looked at every game, and wrote down the name and address of every game company I could find. For the most part, I targeted Milton Bradley, Parker Brothers, and five or ten other large game companies of the day.

I sent them each a letter that basically said, "Hey, I'm a game inventor. I've created this great new game. You guys are going to love it. I'd like to know how I can send it to you or what your policy is for reviewing new games from independent game inventors."

Every one of the companies sent back a letter to me that said something like this: "Hey, do not send us your game. We do not look at outside ideas from unknown inventors. We appreciate your considering us, but if you send it to us, we'll send it back to you unopened."

I thought, why are they doing this? Why wouldn't they want to look at new ideas? I found out why pretty quickly from one letter that elaborated. The reason they don't look at outside ideas from unknown inventors, it explained, was because of the potential for litigation. This particular company had, in the past, looked at and rejected inventions submitted by independent game inventors, and some of those inventors later claimed the company "stole" their ideas.

The large game companies were seeking to avoid any claims of impropriety or theft by having a policy of not looking at outside inventions.

So that was my second effort. My first effort, to approach an invention marketing company, already had not succeeded. I could see now that trying to get a license deal with a manufacturer on my own wasn't going to work either. So then I thought, okay, I need to produce and market the game myself.

How do I do that? I had no idea. But while looking in the *Thomas Register* and other places trying to find a potential licensee, I stumbled across a small company in Chicago called Enjoyable Hour Products.

I'll never forget the company or the owner of the company, a gentleman whose name was Eric Hauser. (While I remember Eric, I don't know if I'm spelling his last name correctly.) In his response to my request for a license deal, he said, "Look, we don't do license deals. In fact, I'm a new publisher and game manufacturer myself. But I can help. I can show you the ropes, mentor you." And so I thought, "Hey, this is great."

I agreed to check out Eric's operation. So I drove to Chicago and met with him. He showed me how to get involved in the manufacturing side of games, how to publish games myself. He showed me how to find the box manufacturers, how to find the manufacturers of game components such as dice or markers, tokens, the Community Chest and Chance like cards that you draw as in a Monopoly game, the simple effort of getting instructions printed.

The help that he provided me was what I needed at the time to move forward. He even helped me find a graphic artist, someone who could do the design and artwork for the game. I hired the artist he recommended.

When I returned home to Detroit, I found a setup box manufacturer and commissioned them to make 100 sample game boxes for me. All the other components for the Dice Baseball game I found elsewhere. I assembled the games in my parents' basement.

I thought with these samples I could again make an effort to find a potential licensee, or I could sell some by mail order and see how they were received.

Chapter 1 - My Story

With the encouragement of my father, I had flyers printed. Then – since Dice Baseball was a baseball game – my father, my sister Phyllis, and I went down to Tiger Stadium during a baseball game and put the flyers on the windshields of cars in the parking lot.

The flyers were simple. They described the game and how "great" it was. An order form was at the bottom of each flyer. Strangely enough, two or three people actually ordered the game. This small success got me excited that people would send me money for my game.

After this small success, I decided to place an ad on TV, a little commercial spot that was basically just slides. I placed a few spots on one of the afternoon movie shows. I got a couple of orders from this as well. While TV advertising was not a sustainable model, I did have fun watching the ads air!

I then placed an ad in the classified section of *The Sporting News*, considered to be "the Bible" of baseball news at the time. I got a couple of orders here as well, which gave me a taste for the mail order business. At the same time I realized that I was spending more on ads than I was making, and that mail order wasn't going to be a sustainable model either.

The Call to Kmart

My next step was to look for a retailer who would put the game on their store shelf.

It was the summer of 1980 when I contacted Kmart. Kmart at the time was probably the largest retailer in the country. They had over 2,200 stores nationwide, and their headquarters were in Troy, Michigan, which was just ten miles from my home in Detroit. I had just turned 21 and was still living with my parents.

I wanted to see if Kmart would carry my game. So I called the headquarters and asked for the buyer of games. They gave me his name and number, I called his office, and I set up an appointment to see him.

Getting the appointment wasn't easy because initially he said, "Why don't you just send me the game" – as many game publishers did at the time – "and I'll review it and get back to you?"

Living only ten miles away from their headquarters, I said, "Rather than send it to you, can I come by and demonstrate it?" He was hesitant but with a little more convincing from me he acquiesced and agreed to meet with me.

By the way, the Kmart buyer's name was George Christensen. As it turned out, he became a mentor and a great help to me as I pursued this effort of getting my games into the marketplace and on store shelves.

I met Mr. Christensen at his office one day in September of 1980. We sat down after shaking hands and exchanging pleasantries. I described the game to him. He took a good look at it. While he didn't actually play it (game buyers don't generally play the games they buy for the retailer they represent; they listen to the descriptions and they go from there), he listened to my description of the game while looking at the packaging and recording his observations on a notepad.

He could see that I was new to the industry. Yet, he helped me a great deal *because* I was green. I didn't know the protocol of the game business. But he could see that I had the *desire* and the *determination* to be successful. So he gave a young kid a chance. He showed me how to package the game for retail, the various forms I needed, and other valuable pieces of information and insight into the game industry. He even gave me samples of other companies' forms so that I could get an idea of the various forms and information I needed to provide retailers. The sample form examples he provided included sale sheets, price lists, and other necessary information.

While Mr. Christensen didn't buy Dice Baseball that year, he did say to me, "Ken, this seems like a pretty good game, and I'd like to give you a chance. However, you have come to me at the wrong time of year. I can't buy any more for this year."

Being new at this business, I didn't know that toy and game buyers at retail companies start doing their Christmas (Fall/Winter) buying earlier in the year, like February or March. In February each year, the Toy Association of America, the industry's national association, sponsors a big trade show in New York City called Toy Fair.

At Toy Fair or soon after, toy and game buyers buy the products or determine what products they are going to buy for the fall – for the Christmas season.

I was seeing Mr. Christensen in September. I didn't know he already had bought his fall and holiday merchandise. So he said to me, "Come see me in March, after Toy Fair, and we'll take a look at it then."

My initial reaction was, "He's just blowing me off to get me out of his office. He's not going to buy my game." And yet I said I would see him then. "Okay, I'll call you in March and set up an appointment."

Meanwhile, I considered other ways I could get my game on the market. I contacted buyers from Sears, Toys "R" Us, and other national chains. They told me pretty much the same thing, "Call me next year after Toy Fair."

So about six months later, in March of 1981, I contacted Mr. Christensen. He remembered me and he remembered my game. He gave me an appointment for early April. I went to see him. I was happy to have another chance at getting Dice Baseball into Kmart.

After my presentation, Mr. Christensen said to me, "Okay, Ken, I'll buy the game from you. However, I can't buy it directly from you because you are not an established business." He added, "I'm not sure you can handle our volume. Do you really have the resources?"

I was 21-years old at this point. After two years of struggling, this was my big break. Mr. Christensen was ready to buy Dice Baseball, to give the game a chance, I thought. But he wouldn't buy it from me as the manufacturer because he didn't believe I could produce it and fulfill the quantities that Kmart would require. The truth is, he was probably right. I'm not sure I was ready at that point either.

So Mr. Christensen said, "Look, if you can find a licensee, I will buy it from them." He continued, "By the way, here are a couple of companies you might want to call." He gave me a list from which I could seek a licensee.

The list included game manufacturing companies that he was already buying products from. "Talk to them. One of them will probably license Dice Baseball from you, produce the game, and sell it to us," he said.

Well, I thought, since the licensee company would pay me a royalty on each game sold, that sounded good to me.

One of the companies on the list was Warren Paper Products, from Lafayette, Indiana. I contacted them by phone, introduced myself, and said, "George Christensen, the buyer over at Kmart, asked me to give you a call to see if you'd be interested in licensing one of my games. It's called Dice Baseball."

They gave me a tentative "Maybe." I continued, "Mr. Christensen told me that if you are willing to license it, he will give you a nationwide order for it." And they said, "Really?"

Now their ears perked up because here they had a potential for a license deal of a product already sold to the largest retailer in the country. It could mean thousands of games sold, tens of thousands of dollars in profit, and little effort on their part, certainly no sales effort because I had already done all the sales. All they had to do was say, "Yes, we'll do it." And, of course, they could sell it to their other retail customers as well.

So Mr. Eggleston, who was the president of Warren Paper Products, invited me to come to Lafayette. We sat down, discussed a license deal, and came to terms for a licensing agreement. A few weeks later, Mr. Eggleston and his vice president came to see me in Michigan to present a draft of their proposed license agreement. We discussed it some more. After a few weeks of negotiating we put together a final license agreement and we signed it.

Kmart immediately gave them the order for a national rollout, and we were off and running. Now I was an "inventor" with a product on the shelf of the largest retailer in the country. I was very, very excited!

I also had a license deal that was going to earn me royalties. Part of my negotiation with Warren Paper stipulated that they had to buy some of the components of the game from me. This allowed me to do what I really wanted to do – be involved in manufacturing, making products, and getting into a real business. I then sourced those components from other suppliers and sold them to Warren Paper. Warren Paper included them in the games, sent the games to Kmart, Kmart paid Warren, and Warren paid me a royalty plus they paid me to purchase those components. So I had a little business going and I was both happy and excited.

Trouble for Dice Baseball

Unfortunately, Dice Baseball did not sell very well. Kmart got their first shipment of the game sometime in August of 1981; in early November, Mr. Christensen told me that they were going to cancel it. I was very disappointed with the failure of my first game!

However, I learned many lessons, most important being that you learn more from your failures than you do from your successes. If you can study your failures, analyze where you fell short, and figure out where you went wrong, you can take that new knowledge, that information, that wisdom, and apply it to your next venture. That's what I did.

One early lesson I learned was that you must do an *evaluation* of your product. Make certain there's a market for it, that people want it, that it solves a problem or fills a need, and that people are willing to pay money for it. I did not do any of that with Dice Baseball.

Remember I said, my brother, my sister, and I played it together for seven years. We *never played it with anyone else*, never even really showed it to anyone other than our parents, so I had no idea if other people would enjoy the game as much as we did. So one of the BIG lessons I learned from the failure of Dice Baseball was to evaluate the market for the idea and test the product or idea with consumers.

Creating Phase 10

One night in December of that same year of 1981, I was visiting my parents, and my sister came home from wherever she had been. She was very excited, bubbling over with enthusiasm. She said, "Hey, guys, I just played this game called Uno. It was so much fun, I went out and bought one."

At her insistence, we all sat down around the dining room table and started playing this card game called Uno. This was the first time I had ever heard of the game, but as we were playing it I quickly realized it played very much like a card game we had played as kids called Crazy Eights. However, the different twists and elements that had been added to Crazy Eights to make it Uno made Uno much more fun than the game we had played as kids.

We played it all evening, laughing and having a good time. I went back to my apartment, where I had moved in April, and started thinking. I did some research and spoke to Mr. Christensen. I discovered that Uno was selling very well. It had been on the market for about ten years and had just experienced its best year in sales during 1981.

Uno was invented by an Ohio barber, Merle Robbins, who initially sold them out of the trunk of his car and in his barber shop. Soon one development led to another and he got a license deal from a company called International Games out of Joliet, Illinois. Uno became a big hit nationwide.

So I thought, card games seemed to be the trend. I'll follow that trend and come up with a card game of my own. My goal, my hope, was that I could develop a card game that would someday compete with or at least become as popular as Uno. I sat in my apartment and thought more. In a few hours, I came up with the idea for what would become Phase 10.

Learning from My Mistakes: Evaluate

In coming up with Phase 10, I knew I had to do things differently than I had done with Dice Baseball if Phase 10 was going to be a success. The first thing I determined to do differently was to do an *evaluation* of Phase 10 before trying to market it, something I did not do with Dice Baseball. Had I done so, I would have known that Dice Baseball was not likely to be a commercial success.

Doing an evaluation meant that I needed to "play-test" it to see what people thought of it. In my initial tests to make sure Phase 10 played as I thought it should play, I would move around a table and play all four hands. I'd move from chair to chair to chair making sure the game played well no matter where I was sitting, all the while trying to ferret out any situations that might come up in the play of the game that required a rule or an instruction on how to deal with it.

After doing that for a day or two, I thought I had pretty much come up with every possible scenario that could come up in the game play. So I wrote the instructions for the game and determined to find out what people thought.

The first people I tested were members of my family: my mother, my father, and my sister. I took the game over to my parents' house. Phyllis, my sister, was still living with them. I gave her the set of instructions I had typed, and I said, "Phyllis, would you read these instructions and then tell us how to play this new game?"

I approached the teaching of the game to them in this way because I figured if I told them how to play the game, they would learn how to play it, of course. But I wouldn't know if the instructions I wrote could be comprehended by the average person without my direct assistance. Obviously I could never sell millions of these games and be in millions of homes explaining how to play it. This was my first test, to give Phyllis the instructions and let her teach us how to play the game. She read the instructions to herself, sat down, and gave us an overview of how to play the game, and we played it correctly.

My second test was to find out if they liked the game. I chose not to ask them directly: "Do you like the game?" I figured that approach would only solicit an "Oh, yes, Kenny, we like the game. It's a good game." They would tell me this, first, because they wouldn't want to hurt my feelings. Second, they wanted to see me successful and would not want to be the ones to crush my dream.

Instead of asking what they thought of the game, I simply observed them and watched for their reactions.

To my joy they were laughing, interacting, using elements of the game to enhance the experience of playing it. I could see that they really liked the game. In fact, they asked to play again! At this point I was thinking I might have a hit! However, I knew I needed to test my game with people who weren't family members.

I Try Again at Kmart

So I performed the same tests with other groups and their reactions were the same. Confidently, I contacted Mr. George Christensen, the buyer at Kmart. I knew he saw something in me he liked, he wanted to help me, and he would at least give my new game a fair review.

I met with him in the spring of 1982 and introduced him to Phase 10, just three months after I started inventing the game, and less than six months after the failure of Dice Baseball. During the time I was marketing Dice Baseball, he taught me how to present a game, how to put together a sell sheet, how to demonstrate the case pack, the weight, and all the information they needed to buy the game. Now I had it all laid out in the "right" kind of presentation. I was better prepared.

By the way, I told him, "This time I don't want to license my game to another company as I did with Dice Baseball. Instead, I want to manufacture it myself and sell it directly to Kmart."

By being better prepared, I gave him more confidence in me. He said, "Okay, Ken, but first, since you are a new company, our volume might overwhelm you if we give you a national order immediately. Secondly, we need to put it out there and test it to make sure it will sell." Of course, I agreed. What choice did I have?

Part 1 - The Inventor Mindset

He said, "I'll put it in twenty stores, and let's see how it does." So he did that. He gave me an order for twenty stores in the metro Detroit area.

Before I left his office, he added, "Ken, you should contact Meijer." Meijer is a regional chain that is headquartered in western Michigan. At that time, they had about fifty stores in Michigan and Ohio. Today they have about 230 stores in six states.

So I did. I called on Meijer and they ordered Phase 10 as well – for all fifty of their stores.

I immediately started contacting component manufacturers. I bought the card decks from a company in Missouri. I bought the game boxes from a company in northern Michigan. The instructions I had printed by a local printer. My friends and family converged in my parents' basement over the course of a couple of evenings to assemble over 2,000 Phase 10 games.

I bought a shrink-wrap machine and we ran the games through it. Shrink wrap is the plastic wrap games are wrapped in so that the boxes stay closed in the stores.

Then we placed the games in shipping cartons and labeled the cartons. My father and I rushed to the UPS airport location – because there were no UPS stores back then – and, on August 10, 1982, we sent out this first shipment to the twenty Kmart stores and fifty Meijer stores.

This was a good start for Phase 10! I had just turned 23-years old nine days prior to the shipment. I had a business actually manufacturing my games. I could see my dream coming true.

Soon after the shipment, some of my friends said to me, "Ken, why don't we go to the twenty Kmart stores and buy all the Phase 10 games over the next week or so? Kmart will think the game is selling well and they'll order more."

While the idea was tempting, I reasoned that, even though the buyer would think the game was selling well and probably give me more orders, *I wouldn't know if the game was selling on its own.* I might get the temporary satisfaction of getting more orders, but my long-term outlook for the game would still be unknown.

Phase 10 needed to prove to Mr. Christensen and me that it would sell! If it did, great. If it didn't, I would move on to my next game invention.

Chapter 1 - My Story

So I nixed my friends' advice and just let the game do its thing. However, what I did do was go to every one of those twenty Kmart stores every week with my clipboard. I took note of the number of games at each location, and compared the number of units present each week with the previous week's numbers. In this way, I was able to determine the sales activity for each location.

I did this for the first month and noted the games were *selling very well*. By the way, it was very exciting the first time I went to a Meijer or, especially, a Kmart store and saw a product that had come from my parents' basement a week earlier on the shelf at "the" major retailer at that time. It was even more exciting to see how well the games were flying off the shelf through sales.

About a month after the first shipment, I reported my findings to Mr. Christensen. Of course, he knew this from his own store reports. He gave me fifty more stores in Chicago. Those fifty stores turned into 800 stores six months later. Eight months later, Kmart put Phase 10 in all their stores. It was given what is called a "basic stock listing," which means it was required to be on the shelf at all times so that customers could always have it available to them to buy. From there, Phase 10 really took off.

I quickly outgrew my parents' basement. I moved production to a warehouse/office setup in a Detroit suburb. I ran the business from there for five or six years, manufacturing and distributing the games all over the country and parts of the world. Then I started licensing Phase 10, including to some international companies.

Phase 10 went on to become a big hit. Now, over thirty-five years later, Phase 10 is still available worldwide. It is currently sold in over twenty-five countries around the world and is available in seven languages. It's the second-bestselling card game in the world, behind Uno.

Mattel has been my licensee since 2010. Mattel is the manufacturer of Uno, Hot Wheels, Barbie, and other toys and games. I have or have had other licensees around the world, including Ravensberger in Germany. Phase 10 is also available as a mobile app.

So I guess I did pretty well in meeting some of my goals when I conceived of the game and going into the game business. I've had other games come and go since Phase 10 was launched but Phase 10 has been my mainstay for all these years.

Part 1 - The Inventor Mindset

Well, that's my story, how I got started, how I got to where I am today. I've been on the venturing side, where my company manufactured games and distributed them to retailers. And I've been on the licensing side, where other companies have done the work for me while I collected royalties.

License or Venture?

Since I have both licensed and ventured, I can advise on both options. You may be at the point where you are not sure which direction to go.

I typically encourage inventors to go the licensing route for two main reasons:

> 1. Most inventors are very good at creating inventions and coming up with ideas but they may not be business people. Being a business person requires a second set of skills most people simply don't have.

> 2. In addition to needing the skill set of a business person if you are going to venture your invention, you need a lot more resources, both financial and otherwise. It can be taxing on the average person who does not have business experience.

However, the advantage of venturing is that you can build a company, a long-term legacy. Also, long term in most cases, you can make more money venturing over licensing. Though that increase in earnings may not be as much as you might think, and certainly not in the beginning.

So it really depends on your skill set. If you've been in business before, if you have a lot of experience in the field that your invention is in, a venture may work for you. But *for most inventors, licensing is probably the better way to go*.

However, another great advantage of venturing is that it gives you a greater chance of getting a licensing deal later on down the road. You can often negotiate a better license deal, including more upfront money and a greater royalty percentage, if you have first ventured and proven your invention will sell.

As you can see, there are upsides to both options. Which way you go really depends on your own individual circumstances. I will discuss licensing and venturing in more detail later in this book.

Chapter 1 - My Story

I ventured because I didn't want to license; I wanted to be in the manufacturing business. That is why it was so critical to me that Mr. Christensen allowed me to sell Phase 10 directly to Kmart, as a manufacturer, rather than license it as I did with Dice Baseball.

He could see that I had a strong desire and was determined to get into the game publishing and manufacturing business so he gave me a chance to do that. Only later did I decide to go into licensing so that I could pursue another business interest in telecommunications and found I couldn't do both businesses at the same time. I was in telecommunications for fifteen years.

Business is in my blood. It was a natural choice for me to venture my inventions; for you it might be different. Licensing is the path that most inventors take. Many of them choose to license because they're tinkerers; they want to be free to create products without worrying about running the business that is going to make and distribute them.

Which route you take depends on your business acumen as well as your own disposition toward business. Being an inventor, though, brings a lot of joy and a lot of satisfaction. I described the joy I felt when I saw my game on the shelf for the first time at Kmart.

You will experience that joy yourself as you create your products and as you see the joy that they bring people whose problems they solve and whose needs they fulfill. The satisfaction you gain is immeasurable.

Chapter 2

Invention Marketing Companies

"Big goals can create a fear of failure.
Lack of goals guarantees it." Unknown

"There is a better way for
everything. Find it!" Thomas Edison

An invention marketing company is a firm that claims they will help you market your invention to manufacturers with the hope of securing a licensing deal with them on your behalf. Invention marketing companies typically work on a fee basis.

Many of them also offer additional services such as:

- Patent application preparation and filing

- Packaging samples

- Product flyers

- Provisional patent application filing, and

- Prototype development

Most of the companies advertise their services on TV, usually late night ads; as well as the Internet, Facebook, Google ads, and other online search engines and social networking sites. They still place ads in the backs of magazines as was their most common manner of advertising back in the 1980's when I first came across them as a young inventor.

While most of these firms have not been shut down completely, many have been fined by the Federal Trade Commission (FTC) for false advertising, making exaggerated claims of success, failing to provide refunds on a timely basis if at all, and a number of other reasons. Others have been in trouble with local and federal agencies, including attorneys general and the Better Business Bureau (BBB).

Part 1 - The Inventor Mindset

Working with Fee-Based Companies

Be very, very careful when you are dealing with any company that operates on a fee basis. Usually, their promise to "assist" you is followed by an agreement or contract that is filled with "disclaimers" outlining how they will do the "best they can" to get your invention on the market while not promising any particular results. What all that means is really the question.

I mentioned Invention Marketing Incorporated (IMI) by name because of my personal experience with them forty years ago. I don't care what they might say about my writing concerning my experience with them at this point. I think they dissolved long ago. However, other such firms that are out there now I won't mention by name. Instead, I will describe how they generally operate and you can decide for yourself what you want to do.

Most people who send in ideas to these invention marketing companies are told that their inventions are great, have huge potential, and, "Oh, by the way, send us five to ten thousand dollars" – or whatever they think the person is capable of paying.

That's how IMI operated and this is how most of these firms operate today. Inventors are charged an initial fee, in some cases nowadays anywhere from $500 to $800, for an "evaluation" or whatever they are now calling it. Other firms charge no fee or very small amounts, less than $100. Then they tell you that you have a great idea and the second fee they ask for is the large one. The second fee request is usually for their assistance in securing a license deal with a – manufacturer. Sometimes they will say the fee is for filing a patent, which usually means a provisional patent and/or for licensing help. Other times, they will offer to make a prototype or retail packaging for this fee.

In most cases they say they will put together a "sell sheet" and a "package" of the product to simulate what the package for the invention might look like on the store shelf. So they'll perform various services but for a *very large* fee.

A friend of mine – this was probably twenty-five years ago – approached me and said, "Ken, I've been dealing with an invention marketing company. They want me to come down to their office here in Detroit. I've already paid them $600 for some initial evaluations, some initial this and that. Now they're asking for money to present it to industry to get a license for me. I want you to come down with me and advise me during their presentation." And so I did.

Chapter 2 - Invention Marketing Companies

On our way there, I warned him, "You know, I don't think you should do this. From my experience and that of other inventors I've dealt with over the years…" – at that time I was probably ten or so years into the industry – "I don't think this is a good idea. Whatever they're promising you – namely, that they will present your invention to the marketplace or to manufacturers in an effort to get you the license deal – you can do yourself and save yourself the $10,000 they want you to give them. It's not that difficult to present your invention to manufacturers." And I promised to help him.

He said, "Well, I've got this appointment. Why don't we go down there anyway?"

So we went to their office and, sure enough, they told him his idea was great. It was wonderful. They then asked if he would be willing to pay the $10,000 fee for their services. I basically nudged him and said, "Hey, let's get out of here."

As we were walking out to the car, I kidded him and continued, "If you just want to give someone $10,000 to send off a few letters to manufacturers, give it to me. It's not that difficult to send a letter." Of course, I'm oversimplifying it; it's a little more involved than that. But not so much that it's worth paying $10,000. I went on to show him how to present his invention to manufacturers himself. He went on to do very well.

Three years ago, a friend approached me with a similar situation. He was working with one of the more widely known invention marketing companies of the day. In this case, he and his partners had already submitted their initial information to the company. As usual, that marketing company had told them it was a great idea.

This friend's idea was a baby product for infants in car seats. While I thought it had potential, I said to him, "Look, there are probably just a dozen or fewer manufacturers of infant car seats in the country. You can contact them yourself and determine if they look at inventions or at outside submissions from inventors. If they do, they'll have a policy and a set of procedures in place to do that. Just follow the procedure and move on from there."

Well, he had a partner who wanted to work with the invention marketing company. Apparently the partner had been totally taken in by the company's hype and he believed that they would help. The $10,000 requested by the invention marketing company, in his view, was a small price to pay because they were going to make "millions." This was "confirmed" by the invention marketing company, or at least they were led to believe that.

My friend decided to go ahead with his partner and they submitted the $10,000 to the invention marketing company. Fast forward two years, the invention marketing company is still "submitting" to manufacturers. They have no deal and it was a waste of money. "I should have listened to you," my friend said to me. "We could've saved 10,000 bucks."

So what's my point here today? I have consulted with thousands of inventors over the years. Many of them came to me *after* they had already submitted money to an invention marketing company. One inventor sent one of these companies over $15,000 for help in getting a license deal that she never got; she wondered if they even attempted to get a license for her. She was on an "easy payment plan," by the way, under which she was to submit $500 a month for several years.

Fee-based invention marketing companies care more about getting the fee than getting you a license deal. If you really are interested in looking at one of those companies, I suggest you look at the website of the Federal Trade Commission (FTC) where you can find information on several of the largest invention marketing companies out there.

How They Stay in Business

How do they stay in business, you wonder? They stay in business because technically they do what they say they're going to do. Let's review what they promise to do.

They say they're going to submit your idea to industry.

That means they will send letters or flyers, maybe make a few phone calls to companies that are appropriate for your particular invention. If you've invented a new bicycle seat, for instance, they will send letters to bicycle manufacturers, and maybe a sales flyer indicating that this invention is available for license. That's what they say they're going to do and, in fact, that is what they do.

They say they're going to file a patent application for you.

Usually they will file a provisional patent application. That's not the same as a utility patent application, which is the full-blown regular patent. A provisional patent application (PPA), which often precedes the regular utility patent application, is not expensive. In fact, the fee for a PPA is less than a hundred bucks for the average person. A utility patent application can cost thousands of dollars in fees and legal expenses.

Exactly what a provisional patent application is, we will cover later in another chapter. For now you need to know this: A provisional patent application is basically a placeholder that sets a priority date for a filing of a "regular utility patent" application that is to follow within one year.

Too often, people don't understand the difference. So when the invention marketing company tells an individual that they're going to "file" a patent application, the person thinks they're going to file a regular patent application, not a provisional application, which is a lot cheaper and *cannot by itself result in a patent*. The company does nothing to dispel the inventor's confusion. Instead they may charge the inventor $4,000 or more, while spending only a few hundred dollars in the application process.

Often the inventor won't find out about this until a year later, if at all.

The invention marketing company does this because they assume the inventor will drop the idea, move on to something else, and not follow through or follow up. If later, through their "marketing" effort, the invention starts to generate interest from potential licensees, they can then request more money from the inventor to pay for the regular patent application, providing some explanation as to why it's needed.

They say they have helped other inventors obtain license agreements.

Yes, they may have had "some" success. However, their success rate, which they don't volunteer, is generally less than 1%. You can ask them their success rate and they are required by law to provide that to you. You'll be surprised!

So, while invention marketing companies generally do what they say, they are not very successful at helping inventors get their inventions on the market. They say they're going to submit your idea to manufacturers, and they do. They say they're going to file a patent application, and they do. They say that they have had some success with other inventors, and they have.

Part 1 - The Inventor Mindset

But when you look at the numbers, you find that about *one in a thousand of the inventors they've worked with have actually gotten license deals*. Of those few who got deals, very few earned enough money through their licensing arrangements to cover all the fees and costs they spent with the invention marketing company.

I could conclude by saying that, for most inventors, it is not a good idea to work with an invention marketing company but I would be hedging. In fact, I think *NO* inventor should work with a fee-based invention marketing company. There are other options and alternatives.

Companies That Can Help

If you don't want to go through the effort of trying to get a license yourself, there are other ways to do it. There are companies that will submit your idea for you on your behalf at *no cost* to you. They simply earn their money off a split of the royalty. Or, if they charge a fee, it is only due upon the successful licensing of the invention. These are companies that are legitimate. You may want to pursue this option.

You can separate the legitimate firms from the bad ones by asking them:

- For their "success" track record

- For references from people they have helped

- For introductions to contact people at one or two of the companies with which they have arranged licenses

In all cases, check them out with the Federal Trade Commission and the Better Business Bureau.

However, if you're savvy enough to come up with an idea and savvy enough to develop it and test it and make a prototype, you are also savvy enough to present it to manufacturers, most of which, if they're willing to look at your idea, will have a procedure in place for you to follow.

It's not hard at all. Later in this book, I'll show you how to do it.

Conclusion

If I had my druthers, fee-based invention marketing companies would not exist because they simply don't tell inventors the truth: Most inventions are not going to be successful. The companies know this and yet take advantage of naïve inventors who think their inventions are "the greatest thing since the toaster." The companies stoke their enthusiasm and take their money through hype, by validating their excitement, even while knowing that the chances of success are slim.

Being aware of this, if you choose to talk to them, approach them with caution, and make sure you get everything in writing if you choose to work with them.

Better yet, I suggest that you don't ever deal with invention marketing companies that are fee based. Don't just walk away from them. Run away from them.

Chapter 3

Inventor "Do's"

"No action, no change. Limited action, limited change. Lots of action – change occurs." Catherine Pulsifer, Author

"Many people have a good aim in life, but for some reason they never pull the trigger." Unknown

It's not enough to think positive. If you want to be successful as an inventor, you have to "do" positive. In this chapter, we're going to discuss the Inventor "Do's," the positive steps that you should be taking in order to achieve success as an inventor. Remember, your goal is to develop your invention, go through the entire process of inventing, and then get it on the market successfully.

You'll get there if you follow these ...

Five Positive Habits for Inventors

1) Take action

2) Join a local inventor club

3) Remain positive

4) Develop more than one idea

5) Review my website for current and continuing information

Let's look at each one individually.

Take Action

If you have an idea swimming around in your head but you've done nothing with it, what's going to happen to it?

1) It will die a slow death in your brain, or

2) Someone else will come up with the same idea, put it on the

market, and make the money that you dreamed of making for yourself.

In order to avoid both of these possibilities, you must move forward. Don't just sit on your idea or let it keep swimming around in your head. Turn your thinking and hoping and pondering into action.

Every incremental development of your idea that takes place in your brain, put it on paper. Make note of the fragments of your idea immediately as you think of them. Put them in order and expand them until you have fully developed your idea.

Then move right into your research evaluation, step 1 of *The Simple Plan* that we will be discussing in more detail later in this book. Cost doesn't have to be a roadblock to action. As we discussed previously, this step doesn't require a whole lot of out-of-pocket cash. A decent research evaluation to find out if your invention has a chance for success often can be done for the cost of copying a few documents, sending a few letters, or making a few phone calls to the appropriate parties.

To take it further, you will use your PC or your laptop to do basic Internet market research. You will do a basic patentability search as well over the Internet. This basic research will cost you little or nothing to determine if you have a commercially, potentially viable invention idea.

Take consistent action. Do something daily to advance your goal of getting your invention on the market. Say to yourself, "Every day, I'm going to do something to advance the commercialization of my invention." It could be a big step for you or a small step but every action matters. They all keep you moving in the right direction, motivated by new signs of advancement and progress toward your goal.

Join a Local Inventor Club

I don't know where you live in the country. Wherever that is, there's a good chance you have an inventor club near you. In the Metro Detroit area, the inventor club is located in one of the suburbs just five miles from where I live.

There are probably six or eight clubs in the state, most of which are within a two-hour drive from me. Two are only an hour away. I've visited five or six of the clubs and found my visits to always be well worth the effort. If you have to drive one hour, one time a month, do it.

Chapter 3 - Inventor "Do's"

To find the inventor club nearest to you, I recommend that you do some research.

Begin with a simple Google search by using the keywords "inventors association" and "[your city or state name]." Searching on "inventors association" and "Michigan," for instance, brings up 18,200 links. You should find inventor groups in the first few pages of search results.

But if you don't, or if you just want to broaden your search, visit the United Inventors Association's website at http://www.uiausa.org The UIA is the national organization established to lobby for inventors' rights and provide basic resources for inventors. At the UIA website you will find a list of the one hundred or so inventor clubs in the United States that are members of the national organization.

At most clubs, from my experience, your first visit is free. After that, member dues range anywhere from $25 to $70 a year. Typically, they hold one meeting a month. The meetings typically last anywhere from an hour and a half to two hours.

You can take advantage of the valuable resources that clubs offer, including networking with the other members themselves. Oftentimes, membership is made up of inventors as well as service providers for inventors. The service providers typically are patent attorneys but may also be engineers, product designers, and developers. In other words, some of the members can help you to develop a prototype locally.

For the meetings, the clubs usually bring in a speaker who is versed in a particular area of concern for inventors. Most of the time, the speakers are service providers for inventors or successful inventors there to tell their success stories and answer the questions of other inventors.

At one local meeting I attended recently, we learned about branding and developing your product and how to get public notice and awareness for it from a speaker who represented a public relations firm. Other speakers were inventors who told their stories of overcoming struggles and obstacles as they worked to get their products on the market. I've given a few of those talks to inventor groups myself around the country.

You will find local inventors who will be able to help you both to create your product and to find resources to develop it.

To summarize, you usually can find inventor clubs by doing a Google

Part 1 - The Inventor Mindset

search. If you can't, go to the United Inventors Association website https://uiausa.org and find the local inventor club nearest you. Ask to see their list of clubs that are part of their association. It is a good idea to attend a few meetings.

So again, I highly recommend you join a local inventor club.

Remain Positive

Keep a positive outlook. This may sound simplistic but it's important because, throughout the process of developing your invention, you are going to run into obstacles. These may include objections from people who don't like what you're doing and negativity from people who tell you your idea is no good and you should quit doing it.

That was my experience. I've lost track of the number of people who warned me that I was wasting my time and my resources trying to get my games on the market.

When I was faced with that type of negativity, I used it as motivation to prove those negative people wrong. I was determined to show them that I could become successful in this business. And I did.

Are you facing similar objections and hurdles? My encouragement to you is to remain positive. Just because you have an invention that may not be successful, may have no market viability, or may already be out there, or your solutions are no better than the current solutions – you still should not become discouraged as an inventor.

Most inventions are not successful. Even products that are actually put on the market are most often dead within a couple of years. Bear in mind that this is all a part of the development process for you as an individual inventor and for your invention.

As you learn to persevere in the face of opposition and discouragement, you become stronger, more determined to think and to tinker and to come up with inventions that do work, while also having real commercial viability.

Thomas Edison once claimed that he constructed three thousand theories while trying to create the light bulb. He had no idea how many different attempts he actually made but it probably was up there in the thousands as well. But even if he failed a mere fifty times, that's more attempts

40

than most people would even come near making before they gave up. He persevered and he learned from those failures.

It's been said that we actually learn more from our failures than we do from our successes. Why? If you are successful in your first effort without facing much opposition, you have no obstacles to test your perseverance. When you face obstacles and persevere against them, you learn, including what adjustments you need to make to reach your goal.

You will learn from your failures. You will learn from those efforts that do not result in successful inventions. Take the information. Apply those lessons to your next invention.

My first venture into the toy and game industry was the baseball board game Dice Baseball; its failure I wrote about earlier. My most important lessons from that experience were to evaluate the potential success of an invention more thoroughly and to evaluate the competition. I applied those lessons to my next invention, which was the card game Phase 10. I didn't make the same mistakes twice. It became a success.

The same can be true for you. After every failure – and you'll have many – take the information you gain and apply it to your next effort, all the while remaining positive and ignoring the naysayers.

Listen to criticism from sources who have knowledge in the field and from potential consumers. Take it constructively. Make the changes necessary and move forward with a positive attitude.

Develop More Than One Idea

You want to develop more than one idea because the chance of any one invention being successful is slim. That's the straight truth.

I could puff you up and tell you, "Hey, you know, every idea you're going to come up with is going to be great. You're going to have a homerun with this one and that one." I could tell you what "inventions marketing companies" do and give you all sorts of positive hype about how successful your invention is going to be—no matter how bad it is.

But that would be a lie and that's not why you bought this book. The truth is, most inventions are not successful. Most patents do not yield a financial return. Get over it. *Confronting and overcoming failure is part of the process of succeeding.*

Part 1 - The Inventor Mindset

If you continue to develop ideas, you will increase your knowledge about the process. You will learn more about the general industry of inventing. You will learn more about the particular industry you're inventing for if you continue to develop ideas within the same industry, which I strongly encourage, especially when you are beginning your career. With your growing knowledge, you will be able to move forward with your second, third, and fourth ideas and each product will get you closer to success.

Here are two reasons why developing products in one particular industry will help you:

> 1) You will advance in knowledge and understanding of that industry. You will learn about market trends, seasonal fluctuations, what the retailers like and don't like, what types of products the market is looking for, how to pitch your ideas, and more.

> 2) You will develop great contacts within that industry. As you go out and seek license deals and talk to distributors and retailers about the particular marketplace niche of your ideas, you develop more contacts. You will meet the people who are doing what you want to do or can help you get to your goals. These contacts will become sounding boards who can look at your ideas, critique them, and help you find your market – or help you to determine that no market exists.

Or, you can develop products for all kinds of industries that are not connected to each another. If you do this, you will have to learn each industry, each trade, each set of buyers, each set of retailers, each set of distributors, each set of manufacturers. Your work becomes much more difficult. While some inventors have found success using this broad approach, I recommend that you confine your inventing energy to one industry, at least for your first few ideas.

A third reason why it is helpful to develop multiple inventions for a single industry is that they will be helpful if you're going to venture your invention. Most retailers prefer to buy more than one product from their vendors. So as a product manufacturer, which is what you are when you venture your invention, you will have a greater chance of success if you can invent more than one product.

When I started out, the buyer at Kmart bought my company's one item, Phase 10. However, he strongly encouraged me to create new games that he could buy. Within a year, I came up with a second card game and he bought it right away. I eventually expanded my line of products within the same industry.

Always try to keep more than one idea going at any given time. Put the second and third ideas temporarily on the shelf while you focus on the first. Take it to the point where it's either ready to launch in the marketplace or you know you have to kill it because your evaluations or your prototypes or your trusted contacts have told you, "You can't launch that invention."

Then pull your second or third idea off the shelf and start working on it.

Whenever an idea of yours doesn't work, remember the words of Thomas Edison: "I have not failed. I have just found 10,000 ways that won't work." Keep working. Come up with another idea, and another. You can do this because you're a creative person, as you've already demonstrated with your first idea.

Review My Website for Current and Continuing Information

My web address is http://www.successfulinventing.com I created it to help you to dive more deeply into all of the ideas we will be talking about in this book, particularly the six steps you need to take in order to successfully take your invention to market:

1) Research Evaluation

2) Prototype Development

3) Product Evaluation

4) Provisional Patent Application

5) Intellectual Property Registration

6) License/Venture

More importantly, through the website, I hold your hand. I add the latest information and services available to the inventing community on a periodic basis.

The website includes:

- Blog: I write a blog with the latest information that I've learned to help you succeed as an inventor.

Part 1 - The Inventor Mindset

- Resources: I provide a list of resources every inventor needs, including:

  - Attorneys

  - 3D printing providers

  - Prototype makers

  - Sample forms, including non-disclosure agreements, license agreements, work-for-hire contracts, and more

- Questions and answers: You can direct your questions to me. I will provide answers or direct you to others who can.

Conclusion

Make success a habit by following these five habits:

1) Take action

2) Join a local inventor club

3) Remain positive

4) Develop more than one idea

5) Review my website for current and continuing information

I want to encourage you to move forward with your invention. The world needs your invention but only you can bring it to the world. So TAKE ACTION!

Chapter 4

Inventor "Don'ts"

"There is a cost and risk to a program of action, but they are far less than the long-range risk and cost of comfortable inaction."
John F. Kennedy

"Nothing will ever be attained if all possible objections must be overcome."
Samuel Johnson

Inventing success means getting your invention on the market and earning yourself an income, whether through a venture or through a license agreement. That's the meaning of success for me. I'm sure that's the meaning of success for you, too.

So this chapter is going to focus on the five inventor "don'ts," those practices that you want to avoid if you want to find success. But, first, let's expose probably the most common myth held by many inventors.

Myth: A Patent Is the Key to Success

Too many inventors think that as long as they have a patent they have the "keys to the kingdom." Well, I'm here to tell you that a patent is not the be-all and end-all guarantee of success. In fact, most products in the marketplace today are not even patented and never were.

A patent merely gives the patent owner the exclusive monopoly right to the patented utility for a period of time. However, a patent does not in itself mean the product will be successful in the marketplace. It only means no one else has a right to the unique patented utility.

By obtaining a patent, many inventors come to believe the patented product will be successful. However, the patent office, as it decides whether or not a patent is warranted, does not examine the market potential of the patented product. It does not "care" about the potential for financial return

45

or gain. It is only examining whether or not the device is unique, novel, or currently claimed in another patent or unpatented invention.

Over 90% of all patents issued – not applied for, but *issued* – by the USPTO to independent inventors do not yield any income to their inventors. At best they yield almost enough to recover the costs of their patents. Most don't even do that.

Many inventors obtain their patents and then frame them and hang them on a wall. I consider that wallpaper, very expensive wallpaper, mind you. That patent can cost you between $7,000 and $10,000, and often more. At one inventors' club meeting, I met a gentleman who claimed to have twenty patents. However, he admitted he had yet to earn any money from his patented inventions, let alone enough to recover the costs of obtaining the patents.

The 5 Inventor "Don'ts"

So my conclusion to the above expensive myth is obvious: Patents are not the be-all and end-all guarantee of success. This leads into my first "don't":

1. *"Don't" run out and apply for a patent prematurely.*

Many inventors tinker, they come up with an idea, and the first thing they do is run out to the USPTO and apply for a patent. Much of their hurry-up attitude is born from the notion that their invention will be stolen and so they need to "protect it." This is unnecessary.

First of all, most ideas are never stolen. Second, you don't need a patent to be successful as an inventor.

However, in a lot of cases a patent is a good idea. So recall this first "don't" but add one word: Don't run out and apply for a patent *prematurely*.

Before applying for a patent, be sure to perform the evaluation steps outlined in *The Simple Plan*. The evaluations will tell you whether or not a patent application is advisable from a market standpoint, from a competition standpoint, and from a patentability standpoint.

Also, you need to determine if you even need a patent based on the complexity of your invention and the cost to build a prototype.

- • **Complexity:** If your invention will be very complex in its manufacturing, it may be a good idea to file a patent application before attempting to proceed with prototyping or manufacturing.

• **Cost:** This factor is usually related to the complexity of the invention. The more complex the invention is, the higher the cost of both a prototype and production units.

If your idea satisfies either of these two conditions, you probably want to get a patent. In a lot of cases though, a patent will not be necessary.

A patent is not necessary, in my view, for products that

> • have a short lifespan (three years or less)
>
> • are fads
>
> • gain high market share quickly

What you want is to be the first one in the marketplace so that, if your invention solves the problem that you hoped it would solve, you can capture a huge portion of that market before anyone else comes along and tries to develop a competing product, because someone will. Whether they "steal" your idea or they just create a new idea that competes with it, if your idea is commercially sound, you will have competition.

A patent isn't necessary to get your idea on the market. A patent only gives you a license to go after someone in court who infringes on your patent. It does not prevent others from putting competing inventions on the market that perform and function differently from your invention but resolve the same problem.

If you do go for a patent, make sure you hire a patent attorney who will do a thorough patent search, before you waste time and money on an application that has no possibility of success. It is a good idea to do a preliminary patent search yourself. You can do this on Google Patents or on the USPTO's Internet site. I discuss this process in detail in chapter 14.

Most patent attorneys will insist on a patent search, but others don't care whether you're wasting your time and money. They will simply prepare your application and submit it to the patent office, not knowing whether or not it has *any chance* of success because they've done no research into its patentability.

In conclusion, don't apply for a regular utility patent until you've evaluated the marketability, the competition, and the patentability of your invention. A patent itself is not a roadmap to success. It's simply a way to prevent others from using your particular technology to solve a problem or need in the marketplace.

2. *"Don't" make your invention public.*

U.S. patent law gives you one year from the day that you make your patent public to apply for a regular utility patent. Public exposure starts the clock ticking. If you have not applied for a patent by the time a year expires from that first public exposure, you will lose your rights to obtain a patent and your invention will come into the public domain. That would mean anyone can produce it. So don't make your invention public if you intend to apply for a patent at some undetermined point.

Another reason for not making your invention public is so that you can keep it confidential until you have done all of the evaluations necessary to determine if it has commercial possibility. By keeping it confidential, no one else knows that you're working on a specific solution to a specific problem. If you consider something is a problem, others probably do as well. You want to come up with the solution before they do.

But, and this is what makes it interesting, part of the evaluation process requires you to ask others what they think, and the "others" could include possible consumers or competitors of your invention. How do you protect yourself from them?

There are two ways. First, in asking for their opinions do not talk about your specific solution. Ask only about the problem:

- Have you experienced this problem?

- What product are you currently using to resolve that problem?

- Would you be willing to pay for a solution to the problem?

- How much would you pay for a solution?

- How much have you paid in the past for a solution? Do you know others who experience the problem and are in need of a solution?

- If you don't have a solution to the problem, why? Is it the cost or a lack of solutions in the marketplace?

In this way, you keep the specific details of your invention confidential.

Non-Disclosure Agreement (NDA)

Second, you are, nevertheless, exposing the fact that you're coming up with an idea to resolve that particular problem. Therefore, require everyone you share this information with to sign a non-disclosure agreement (NDA).

In signing an NDA, they are saying that they will not make the information that you share with them public. They'll keep it confidential so you can keep your invention secret for as long as possible. This will reduce the risk of someone else beating you to the market with a similar solution.

You also avoid potentially ruining your patent possibilities. Remember, from the day you make your invention public, you have one year to file a regular patent application. Otherwise you will lose your right to file for a patent forever.

I provide an example of an NDA on my website www.thesimpleplan. com Check it out.

Although most individuals reviewing your idea will not offer much resistance to signing your NDA, some individuals or companies will. For some, it is a general reluctance to deal with "inventors." You can avoid this reluctance from the start by never referring to yourself as an inventor; rather, refer to yourself as a "product developer." When you put yourself in this different light, they are more likely to view you as a professional and as such, they will drop their guard and sign.

Other companies may not want to sign your NDA, but they would rather you sign their NDA. In this case you will have to review the proposed NDA and decide whether or not you want to sign it. In my opinion, signing their NDA usually is not a problem. However, if you see something in the agreement you don't like you can ask for it to be removed or altered. If that doesn't work, you must either go with their NDA or seek to work with your other prospects. If nothing works out with the other prospects, you can always come back to this one as a last resort.

So again, keep your idea as confidential as you can. Avoid public exposure. Don't put it up for sale in any form. Don't expose it to the general public through the Internet or other forms of social media ... until you've determined that your invention merits your continued pursuit and has commercial possibilities. Always approach inventing with a view toward professionalism. Then move forward to the next step in *The Simple Plan*.

3. *"Don't" become paranoid.*

You never want to become a paranoid inventor. As a paranoid inventor you are afraid to talk about your idea. You become fearful that everyone is going to *steal* it. You imagine there are people lurking in the shadows or looking over your shoulders trying to figure out what you are doing, how you are doing it, and how they can get their hands on it.

As we discussed before, that likelihood is small. Most inventors have heard horror stories of ideas being stolen. But, in reality, companies and individuals don't steal ideas. They steal proven, successful products, not *ideas* for a new product.

Even if they like your solution and they think the whole world will beat a path to your door to buy it, are they willing to take the risk of producing it, developing it, going into manufacturing, and getting it distributed? Are they willing to spend all the money necessary to get it out there? In most cases they are not.

More likely, a company or individual who is excited about your invention will be a good candidate as a licensee. There is less risk for them. They don't have to worry about their reputation being sullied because they've been accused of stealing ideas.

So until your invention is out there in the marketplace making a lot of money, you don't have much to worry about. Could it be stolen? Perhaps. Is it likely? No.

So, don't become a paranoid inventor. Don't develop the negative mindset of paranoia.

4. *"Don't" beat a bad invention.*

You've heard the expression, "Don't beat a dead horse." I call this "beating a bad invention." I'm talking about the inventor who has poured heart and soul into creating an invention. Now, in spite of all the warning signs out there that it has no commercial possibilities, that the marketplace does not want that invention, the inventor continues to spend money and time and effort on it.

You want to avoid this mindset.

What are the warning signs that it's time to let your idea go?

- It's too expensive and the market will not pay the price.
- The technology to make it is too far ahead of its time.
- The competing solutions are superior to yours.
- The consumer just does not understand your invention.

You may say, "What does it mean that they don't understand it?" Remember, your solution must be simple enough for the average consumer to utilize. Most people want simplicity. They want a product that works every time. They want it to be effective and efficient. And they want it to be competitively priced.

But if the functionality of your invention is too complex for them to operate and they don't understand how to use it, or if they aren't clear how it will benefit them, they won't buy it.

These are times when an inventor may "beat a bad idea." Don't be that inventor. Let it rest. Move on to your next invention.

I've met inventors in groups and clubs around the country who have been "working" on their inventions *for years*. One gentleman I met said he had been working on his for ten years. As he was bragging how much time and effort he had put into developing and testing and working on it, I was thinking to myself, "This is not a good idea."

I thought, "If it has taken you ten years to develop it, either the market is telling you they don't want it and you're ignoring the warning signs, or you haven't done a research evaluation so you have no idea what the market wants. If you don't ask the market you are putting yourself in potential financial danger by expending time, resources, and money on an invention without the vaguest idea whether or not it will sell."

So I asked him, "Have you done any market research of your invention"? In response, the man admitted that he had never asked the "market" if his invention was a product it wanted. He never evaluated the market potential. He assumed that the market would love it. He is still "working on the invention" to this day.

He suffers from one of the classic inventor negative mindsets I'll outline in a coming chapter: "empty-nester syndrome." Instead of developing their ideas as quickly as possible and getting them into the marketplace, inventors suffering from this "ailment" unconsciously stall, delay, and do everything they can to slow the process while at the same time continuing to "work on it." The reality is, they don't want to let it go. They never get it out to the marketplace because the "act" of inventing is more important to them than bringing it to life. Essentially they turn their inventions into their hobbies, not potential profit-making endeavors.

So don't beat a dead invention. This means:

- Don't "work" on your invention endlessly.
- Don't pursue an invention that the market is telling you it does not want.
- Don't pursue an invention that you have not fully evaluated to determine if, in fact, it *will sell*.

You must determine whether or not it *will sell* as early in the process as possible to save yourself time and resources, and, of course, a lot of frustration.

5. "Don't" spend money needlessly.

Most inventors are concerned, with good reason, about the spiraling costs they will face to get their inventions to market. Yet, in their excitement to get to market, they spend money needlessly. Don't do it. You may respond, "Ken, that goes without saying. I'm not going to waste a lot of money on this invention."

Well, you'd be surprised how many inventors waste time and money on inventions that are going nowhere.

Most of the money that you're going to spend on your invention following *The Simple Plan* occurs *after* the research evaluation you do in step one to determine whether you should even move on to step two. I've already shown you how this first step need not cost you much money, if any money at all. Much of the research evaluation process you can do yourself for the price of a few postage stamps or the cost to copy a few sheets of paper. Your biggest investment at this stage will likely be your time and effort. It's not difficult if you're willing to do the work.

The evaluation itself is no guarantee that your invention will be successful, which means that it will sell. But it is your best indicator whether or not you should move to step two, where costs begin to accumulate as you create the prototype.

A prototype can be created inexpensively depending on your invention. In some cases you can cobble together a functioning prototype from other products. I did this with Phase 10. I took cards from other games to make up a complete deck of the cards needed to play Phase 10. I made an example of the Phase 10 game box by turning the box of an Uno card game inside out. I now had a white box. I placed the graphics for Phase 10 on the box. I then placed the Uno cards back into the box and sealed it. This gave me what appeared to be a "production" copy of Phase 10. Producing this prototype only cost me about $1,500. Most of that cost was the fee I paid to the artist for the graphics. Today, with modern computers and graphics programs, I could make that prototype for even less.

Prototypes of more complex inventions will cost more. However, with the growth of 3D printing, it's getting cheaper and cheaper to make prototypes. Simple inventions, those that have few or no moving parts, can be prototyped via 3D printing for just a few hundred dollars.

So again, don't spend money needlessly. Be cautious. Don't pay patent attorneys before you've performed the necessary steps to determine if your invention will sell.

Quick Review

Okay, now, those are the five "don'ts." Let's review:

1. Don't run out and apply for a patent prematurely.

Just be cautious. Do whatever is necessary to determine whether your invention will "sell" before you spend $10,000 or $20,000 on a patent.

2. Don't make your invention public.

Have everyone who you disclose your invention to sign a non-disclosure agreement so you can preserve your marketability and your patentability.

3. Don't become paranoid.

Don't become a paranoid inventor or develop a negative inventor mindset. Paranoid inventors never get their inventions on the market because of their fear of everyone and every step of the process.

Part 1 - The Inventor Mindset

4. Don't beat a bad invention.

If all signs are saying your invention will not sell or if the invention becomes so costly to produce that you can't find investors, stop and move on to something else.

5. Don't spend money needlessly.

Conserve your cash. Be guided by the results of your research evaluation and look for inexpensive solutions as you begin to spend money creating your prototype.

These are the five "don'ts," the negative practices that hold back your progress. Giving in to them will make your inventing process more difficult and expensive as you try to move forward.

If you avoid them, you will be much more equipped and ready to be a successful inventor.

You may have in your mind right *now* an invention that can help you reach your financial goals, enable you to spend more time with your family and friends, and take a vacation around the world. Whatever your dreams may be, you may have that invention in your mind right *now* that can get you there.

Be mindful as an inventor that you want to maintain a positive mindset as you go forward. That's the subject of the next chapter.

Chapter 5

Maintain a Positive Mindset

"When it is obvious the goal cannot be reached, don't adjust the goals, adjust the action steps." Confucius

"Worry is the misuse of the imagination." Dan Zadra

Your mindset is the attitude that you bring into any situation including life in general. Your mindset determines your outcome. Garbage in; garbage out. Your mindset is the established set of attitudes you hold.

You can choose to have a positive mindset or a negative mindset. In this chapter I'm going to show you how to maintain a positive mindset and why. In chapter 6, I'll show you how to avoid the negative mindset and why.

Focus

To be a successful inventor you must have the ability to focus your efforts on your mission of creating your product and bringing it to the marketplace. Distractions are everywhere and must be avoided or controlled.

These distractions can come in many forms. They can be the everyday cares of life, such as trying to earn a living, rearing and caring for children, and attending to the needs of others. You can't avoid these distractions since they are a part of your responsibility if you are married with or without children.

Other distractions you must avoid, including excessive seeking of entertainment and leisure. Even your normal amount may have to be reduced or sidelined for a time while you work to bring your invention to market.

If you are a procrastinator who starts projects and doesn't finish them, you'll have a difficult time being an inventor. An inventor must come up with the idea and then move as quickly and effectively and efficiently as possible to get it onto paper, then into a prototype stage, and finally onto store shelves.

Timing is of the essence. You don't want to see someone else come out with your idea and get it on the shelf before you. No one else will, if you maintain your focus and keep your drive in the right direction.

Deal with Setbacks

You will face setbacks and other difficulties. One difficulty I faced when I started out was in trying to come up with the seed money to manufacture my games. When Kmart gave me what was at the time my largest order ever, for my Phase 10 card game, I was publishing and manufacturing the games myself; I wasn't licensing yet. So I needed to come up with $20,000 to pay the manufacturer of the cards so that they would produce the order. I didn't have anywhere near that kind of money.

Initially, I looked to the bank for a loan but, because I was only in my early twenties, the bank turned me down. The loan officer said that, while my personal credit rating was good, I didn't have enough time in the business.

I have forgotten how many units Kmart ordered, but, since I needed $20,000 to make the games, I imagine it was somewhere between 20,000 and 30,000 games. Remember, we are talking about the early 1980's! That was a lot of money back then.

I thought of my friends and family but concluded that all of them together couldn't loan me that much money. So I called the CEO of the company that made the card decks for Phase 10 and asked him to extend me a line of credit.

Although my personal credit was good, my business didn't have any credit with manufacturers at that time as I always paid COD. This time, I asked the CEO to give me credit terms with 30 days to pay. Meanwhile, he would ship me the order of cards so I could assemble the games and then ship them to Kmart.

The manufacturer said no, he wouldn't extend credit terms of any kind to me. His view was the same as the bank's view: I was new in the business and in my dealings with him and he was afraid that he wouldn't be paid.

I began to think creatively. I thought, if he won't give me the credit because I'm new, maybe he will give the credit to Kmart, which at the time was a good credit risk.

Chapter 5 - Maintain a Positive Mindset

I contacted the card company owner again. I conceded to him that I understood why his company couldn't extend the credit to my business. But, I asked, would he consider extending the credit to Kmart? He said to me, "Well, Ken, of course! We will extend the credit to Kmart, but how is that going to happen? You're the one buying the cards from us."

I said, "That's true, but if I can get Kmart to pay you directly for the cards with the first $20,000 of the first payment that they will owe me, would you agree to that?" He said to me, "If you can convince Kmart to pay me directly, I will agree to your terms and get your cards out to you right away." I said, "Great."

Now, here I was with an agreement with the manufacturer of my cards. This was not the complete game, by the way. He simply manufactured the decks of cards. I still needed to get the instructions and the "tuck" boxes printed. Then we had to assemble them in my basement "warehouse,", shrink-wrap them, package everything, and deliver them to Kmart.

But the cards were the major component of the game. With this agreement, I now had to convince Kmart to pay him directly. I didn't know whether or not they would do that.

I called Mr. Christensen, the buyer at Kmart, and I said, "I've got a little bit of a problem and maybe you can help me with it." He said, "Sure. What can I do?"

I said, "My card manufacturer in Missouri cannot extend credit to me because my company is new and a new customer of their firm." He said he understood.

I continued, "I came up with a creative way of getting him paid but I need Kmart to help me." He said, "What do you need?"

I laid out my plan for Kmart to pay the card company directly off the top of my invoice. "Instead of paying the first $20,000 to me, pay it to them and then pay me the balance. I know there may be some paperwork hassles, but I need this in order to get going." He said, "Sure, no problem."

I thought, "Did I hear him right?" He repeated, "Ken, that's no problem at all."

He explained, "Basically, you're talking about factoring. We factor invoices all the time." Here, I thought I was creating a new way to finance a

57

Part 1 - The Inventor Mindset

business, yet there was a program called "factoring" of receivables that has been in existence since who knows how long and it's a common practice. Although my arrangement was not traditional factoring, it resembled it.

In a factoring arrangement, when I send an invoice to my customer, in this case Kmart, the factor, the company that financed me, is paid the invoice amount by the customer. Then, the factor takes back, with interest, the money I owe them and pays me the invoice balance.

What I was proposing was a variation on a factoring arrangement. Therefore, Kmart had no problem with it.

The reason I tell you this story is to reinforce my belief that, if you give yourself the time to sit and think through your challenges, you will likely come up with a solution. However, creating and thinking up those ways to circumvent obstacles requires a positive mindset.

Maybe the challenge involves your invention itself. Maybe it doesn't perform the way you expected. Maybe the components or materials that you envisioned were necessary to create the invention don't hold up under stress, pressure, or heat.

Whatever the situation, as an inventor, you must maintain a positive mindset to allow your creativity to come up with solutions to your challenges. Rather than give up and quit, you have to see before you a challenge that you know you will overcome. Your positive mindset is focused, driven, and determined to see this adventure through to the successful end.

Thomas Edison-like Determination

I wrote earlier about how Thomas Edison failed hundreds of times before he successfully created the light bulb. As you can imagine, he faced many challenges and failed at all of them, until he succeeded.

As an inventor, you face similar challenges. Sometimes, your invention does not function well initially and you need to create a new way to make it work. The question is, "How will you face that challenge?" Will you allow negativity to blot out your vision and creative drive? Or, will you have Thomas Edison-like determination?

Chapter 5 - Maintain a Positive Mindset

If It's Not Viable – Move On

I've described the positive mindset as the ability to face challenges, move forward, and not be discouraged easily. At the same time, you have to take constructive criticism and put it to use. If you find during the evaluation process that your invention has no commercial viability, for whatever reason, then your positive mindset allows you to change course.

You must put that invention on the shelf and move forward with another one. If you're the kind of inventor that I suspect you are, you probably have more than one idea swimming around in your head. If Idea A turns out *not* to be commercially viable, for whatever reason, move on to Idea B, and then C.

Remain positive. Remain focused. Have Thomas Edison-like determination. Don't be easily discouraged. When I was creating my games initially, friends told me that there was no money in making games. They said, "You can't be a success."

What I discovered was that people who discourage you and tell you that you can't be successful often are reflecting their own negative self-images. They feel they can't do it so they believe you can't do it either. Don't let them discourage you.

When people tell me I can't do something, I actually become emboldened and more determined to prove them wrong. You can, too.

There are really two sides of being an inventor: the side that creates an invention and the individual invention.

You may call yourself an inventor, and, in fact, you are, even if you create only products that are not commercially viable. But a successful inventor creates successful products.

Successful inventors also create unsuccessful products – but they know when to let them go. They know that most inventions will not be successful and that every failure gets you one step closer to success as you maintain a positive mindset and move forward with your other ideas.

Chapter 6

Avoid a Negative Mindset

"I couldn't wait for success, so I went ahead without it."
Jonathan Winter

"A person going nowhere can be sure of reaching his destination."
Unknown

Now let's discuss the negative side of the inventor mindset. Unfortunately, I have discovered nine negative mindsets that entrap too many inventors and prevent them from ever getting their inventions on the market.

They are:

1) Inventor Paranoia

2) The Omnipotent Inventor

3) The Greedy Inventor

4) The Impatient Inventor

5) Empty-Nester Syndrome

6) The Emotional Inventor

7) The Deaf Inventor

8) The Procrastinating Inventor

9) "Look, Ma, Top-of-the-World" Syndrome

Inventor Paranoia

Inventor paranoia is probably the most common negative mindset that inventors have. Many successful inventors have written about it.

Part 1 - The Inventor Mindset

The paranoid inventor is fearful that someone will steal their idea. They lose their focus and their ability to think straight. They act in ways that can be unnecessarily costly to them.

Running to the patent office and seeking a patent before it's necessary or advisable is one example. We will discuss patents and the advisability of getting one later in this book; for now let me just say that getting a patent prematurely is costly and can have a negative effect on the long-term potential success of your invention.

Let's take a look at this form of paranoia.

What is really the likelihood of someone stealing your invention idea? Most inventors have heard horror stories of inventions being stolen by companies or individuals. I'm here to tell you it generally *does not* happen.

I have seen thousands of inventions and heard from thousands of inventors, all with many ideas; none that I can recall had legitimate claims of idea theft, though I don't doubt it has happened.

Most "inventions" are just ideas in the head of the inventor. Companies don't steal ideas. No one knows if an "idea" is going to be successful. Most of the time when you hear of an idea being stolen, what you are really hearing about is an invention or product being "knocked off" or "counterfeited."

A counterfeit is a cheap imitation of a successful product. From afar, it looks like the original product but, upon closer inspection, differences, often flaws, are easily discovered.

For instance, Uno, the number one commercial card game in the world, is produced by Mattel. When a company other than Mattel produces their own version of the game, designed and packaged to look and feel like the version produced by Mattel and sold as though it is the original, the "infringing" company, usually from Asia, is producing a counterfeit. I was at an outdoor flea market and saw several vendors selling Uno counterfeit. I knew they were counterfeit because, upon close inspection, I noticed several discrepancies in the packaging.

A knockoff can be, using the example of Uno, a game that is essentially the same as the original but has a different name.

In both cases, the companies are committing criminal acts. There are penalties.

Does this frighten you? It shouldn't. Counterfeits and knockoffs only happen to "successful" products. Companies make these products because they know they can sell them without having to take the risk of investing in the R&D phase.

For instance, companies all over the world sell imitations of Louis Vuitton bags. They look like the real thing, but on close inspection, you can usually discover features that show that they are fakes, and usually of inferior quality. You might find that the stitching or the chain is slightly different. The leather may be of poorer quality. In one or more ways, it doesn't meet the quality standards of the original because the companies that are producing the knockoffs usually cut corners wherever they can to reduce costs.

The point here is that counterfeits and knockoffs only happen to successful products. Disreputable companies steal successful products. They don't steal ideas or unproven products because no one knows if they will prove to be successful products.

Reputable companies like Mattel or General Motors or Johnson & Johnson don't steal ideas at all because they don't want their reputations ruined in the marketplace. Mattel, who I know well because they manufacture my Phase 10 cards games, does not look at outside ideas from unproven inventors for fear that they will be accused of stealing the ideas.

Also, introducing new brands into the marketplace is risky. So they prefer to either buy proven products from smaller companies or create products based on license deals; for instance, if Star Wars has a new movie, they will create a product based on the Star Wars characters under a license agreement with the owners of the brand.

So those are reasons to keep in mind why you should avoid inventor paranoia. Of course, you want anyone who has seen your idea to sign a non-disclosure agreement to protect you and keep it confidential. But for the most part, don't be afraid to talk about your invention *under the right circumstances of confidentiality.*

In fact, you *must* talk about it in order to determine if it has commercial viability.

Part 1 - The Inventor Mindset

The Omnipotent Inventor

Omnipotent inventors think they can do everything. They don't need anyone's help or advice. They've got it all covered.

This attitude can be a problem because as an inventor you will need to seek advice and support from others who have expertise in the field of your invention.

Having said this, if you don't want to bring someone else in as a partner, you must be careful about utilizing their ideas or suggestions in your invention. If you use someone's suggestion as an element of your invention, you may be required to share the patent and a portion of the profits with them. I usually don't ask for suggestions when seeking feedback. Instead, I say I merely want to know their view of "my" invention. I don't seek their ideas to enhance it in any way. Thus I avoid someone claiming part ownership of my inventions.

So the omnipotent inventor thinks it's possible to do anything and everything, wear all the hats, not just for the invention itself, but including building a company, venturing the invention, and more.

Avoid this mindset. Don't become the omnipotent inventor. Seek help and guidance where you need it and be willing to take the advice of those who have expertise in your field.

The Greedy Inventor

The greedy inventor is one of the most common of all the negative mindsets.

Greedy inventors feel the need to hoard every dollar that comes from their inventions. They don't want to set up partnerships even when they are necessary because partnerships mean giving up certain profits. They don't hire brokers to assist with license deals because broker payments are paid out of the royalty.

Another common area where I see inventor greed is when an inventor will not sign a license deal with a potential licensee unless the licensee offers some kind of upfront payment. The greedy inventor may request an upfront fee of $100,000 or more.

Insisting on or asking for too much money upfront can make your invention prohibitive for the manufacturer, the potential licensee, to produce profitably and threaten the whole deal because it puts them too far in the hole in advance of a product that's unproven. Having said this, there are circumstances where negotiating the payment of money upfront makes sense and is appropriate.

For example, an upfront fee may make sense as a recovery of patenting expenses, or to reimburse you for inventory you've already purchased. Anytime the licensee will benefit also, it may make sense for them to pay a fee upfront. If the fee only benefits you, you may risk alienating your potential licensee.

So, you have to avoid being greedy in your efforts to get money upfront. Most manufacturers will not pay high upfront fees and will therefore reject a license of your invention.

The Impatient Inventor

The impatient inventor is not willing to wait and see the invention through the normal process.

This inventor does not give the potential licensee sufficient time to determine if, in fact, they can work with this product or will want to license it. Instead, the inventor pushes too hard, insisting on immediate results. This attitude may cause potential licensees to drop out of the deal because they are not given the time to use their resources to investigate the invention's potential.

So avoid this mindset by first giving your potential licensee enough time to review your invention. This may take a couple of months on average. Pin them down on how long they need to review it and then hold them to that. During this review time they are likely checking the market of the invention and their ability to capture a share of it. They will also review the manufacturing side of the invention, the cost of manufacturing, distribution channels, the intellectual property (IP) rights, and perhaps other factors.

If the review goes beyond the allotted time, you may either request they come to a decision, give them more time, or consider seeking a different licensee. Just don't allow impatience to rule the day.

Empty-Nester Syndrome

Inventors who suffer from empty-nester syndrome are those who basically do not want to let go of their inventions and hand them over to interested licensees. They just can't let go. It's like they are afraid of letting their "baby" grow up and move out of the house. This syndrome will cause the inventor, even one with a good, viable invention, to miss out on profiting opportunities.

As an inventor myself, I understand that when you've spent a long time – in my case over forty years – building a brand, it's hard to imagine giving it up to someone. On the other hand, I was willing to do that under the right circumstances.

At the time I started licensing Phase 10, I had been producing and selling it nationally for over five years. I enjoyed the business side of manufacturing the games and took pride in the business I had built. However, I realized I could extend the brand even further through licensing. I did not let the fear of "letting go" impede the growth and progress of the game.

Through licensing, I was able to gain international partners who could produce and sell the games all over the world. Also, my licensee for the United States was able to get the games into U.S. retailers where I could not. That extended the game's growth in the United States and also in Canada. As a result of increased retail sales, I was making more in royalties than I was making operating as the game's manufacturer.

I also now had the freedom to pursue other business ventures that have yielded more income for me and my family. I don't regret "letting go" at all.

By licensing, an inventor can avoid all of the risks and problems associated with business operations and simply sit back and earn royalties. Also, you can take advantage of the resources the licensee has to offer.

Avoid the empty-nester syndrome at all costs.

The Emotional Inventor

The emotional inventor is similar to the empty-nester in that this inventor is so wrapped up emotionally in the invention that it comes to feel like part of the inventor, a reflection of the inventor's soul.

Beware of this dangerous attachment because there may be a time when you will need to either sell it outright or license it. In both cases, you must let go, relinquish control, a situation many empty-nesters and emotional inventors just can't handle. As a result, they subconsciously avoid, and therefore miss out on, potentially lucrative licensing deals.

The Deaf Inventor

The deaf inventor doesn't listen, doesn't hear any advice, any critique about his or her invention. Instead, this inventor turns a deaf ear to any opposing ideas.

Inventors who don't listen to sound advice from industry experts, from potential licensees, or from current licensees on how to proceed with their invention often find themselves in a difficult position that may cause them to lose the deals they have, including licensed deals or, if they are manufacturers, their customers. Examine yourself and make sure that you are not deaf when it comes to advice regarding your invention.

How can you determine whether or not you are a deaf inventor? Well, ask yourself, do I make adjustments as advice seems to require? Have I ignored the advice of customers related to my invention and any changes the majority may require? Have I ignored the advice of retailers related to my product packaging, size, and other features? Am I pursuing an invention the market is telling me it doesn't want?

Over the years I've seen many inventors ignore sound advice from potential customers and industry experts to pursue inventions that are going nowhere. This can lead to many problems including lost money in the vain pursuit.

The Procrastinating Inventor

Then there is the procrastinating inventor. Procrastinating inventors just never really get around to completing their inventions. Or they never quite get around to finishing their prototypes or testing them thoroughly. They never quite get around to following up on interest from potential licensees. They just procrastinate and never get things done.

Then, when they see what they think is their invention idea on the shelf somewhere, they say someone "stole" their idea. The reality is, if your invention truly solves a pervasive problem or fills a widespread need, someone else out there, whom you may not even know, is probably working on a solution to the same problem.

Time doesn't slow down to wait for the procrastinating inventor.

Part 1 - The Inventor Mindset

"Look, Ma, Top-of-the-World" Syndrome

This affliction is demonstrated by the inventor who *must* be the head of a venturing operation. Otherwise, they will not pursue their invention. They see themselves as being capable of starting and running a business that will grow into one of "world domination" as it relates to their invention.

I've seen over the years several examples of this in inventors. Most recent is an inventor who has created a remarkable invention that could revolutionize the way high-volume manufacturers reduce scrap and rework in their manufacturing processes. The best advice from all sources told him that, due to his inexperience operating a business of any kind, he should bring on an experienced CEO to head the operation.

Well, he rejected that advice. As a result, the business is suffering greatly and his investors are facing the total loss of their investments.

Don't let this happen to you! Oftentimes, the inventor is not the same person to successfully market the invention or lead the company producing the product. Due to a lack of business experience, the inventor may not be the person to head the venturing company.

So avoid the "Look, Ma, top-of-the-world" syndrome by being willing to hand over the venturing operation to the person best equipped to lead the business, and your invention, to success.

Conclusion

So those are the nine negative mindsets I've seen inventors display. I want you to avoid them. Continue to work hard; continue to move forward with your inventions.

Don't let negative inventor mindsets cause you to delay or to lose a licensee or a deal, because you've become greedy or emotionally attached to your invention.

It's okay to talk with the appropriate people about your invention, for input, advice, consultation, and assistance. In fact, it is advisable. Just be sure to require those you discuss your invention with to sign an NDA to help you keep your invention confidential.

Be willing to let the invention go, unlike the empty-nester or the emotional inventor. Let the people who are experts in the field, license your invention or get it in the marketplace and do what they think is necessary to make it a success. They know their industry; they know what they are doing. If you've chosen them wisely, they will take it and make it a true success. Let them do their job.

But be cautious about asking for upfront payments. I'm not going to tell you it's not going to happen. Just avoid being greedy. Don't blow a deal over an upfront-fee request because more often than not they do not work.

Many inventors have destroyed the potential of their invention by giving in to the various "negative mindsets" I have discussed here. Don't let this happen to you. Move forward. Continue to maintain a positive mindset.

Always be reasonable about your invention. Stay healthy!

Chapter 7

Idea Development

"I've failed over and over and over again in my life and that is why I succeed." Michael Jordan

"Well done is better than well said." Ben Franklin

You may not yet have an invention in mind or perhaps you've gone to the point of making a prototype and testing it. Maybe your invention is still just an idea swirling around in your head.

In this chapter, we're going to discuss how to develop an idea. You're going to learn what types of ideas or inventions are *more likely* to be commercially successful and generate real income for you versus those that are not.

Getting Started

The first thing you want to do is find or develop an idea that:

- solves a serious problem, or
- fulfills a need

The method that people currently use to deal with a problem or need may be ineffective or not efficient in bringing about the resolution that they want. They are looking for a "better way" – or they would be attracted to one if you offered it.

For example, it's much more effective and efficient to drive a nail into a piece of wood with a hammer than it is to use a rock or a piece of plastic or the end of a screwdriver. While a rock will do it, the hammer solves this problem more effectively and more efficiently.

Part 1 - The Inventor Mindset

Filling a need can be as simple as providing a means of entertainment or recreation. That's what my games do.

Your idea can be the hammer that drives the nail efficiently and effectively, or it can be the diversion that provides entertainment, relaxation, and recreation.

Now, if you have an idea that you haven't fully developed yet, or if you don't yet have an idea, ask yourself:

- What problem does this idea solve or do I want to solve?
- What need does it fill or do I want to fill?

If your invention doesn't solve a problem that a large number of people have, you're not likely to have much success. If you find a small minority of people who have that problem, you can make money with your invention only if that niche is large enough, and if they perceive that they have a real problem and are willing to pay money for your solution.

Niche Product Example

Let me give you an example of this. I was meeting with an inventors' group in Michigan in early 2015. Some of the inventors were showing off their ideas, which included prototypes as well as products that they had actually created.

One gentleman was in the excavating business; he saw a problem that only excavators have. Now, it's not a problem I would have recognized, and unless you were in that business you probably wouldn't have recognized it either. But because he was in the business, he realized that this particular problem was widespread within the niche of ground excavation.

The problem arose when operators of excavation equipment worked on surfaces that were not level and tilted a certain number of degrees. This situation made it difficult for them to determine balance and digging angles. The problem was serious enough for that niche community that people in the business over the years had cobbled together their own "homemade remedies" and solutions. None were completely satisfactory.

So the gentleman came up with his own solution. It was a globe-like device that contained a leveling type of system that made it possible to determine the angle and degree of your pitch. He was showing it to everyone in the audience and they were looking and commenting and asking questions.

Not being excavators, we didn't know that there was a problem. However, the inventor not only knew that there was a problem but that it was recognized in the industry because he had surveyed other excavators and they had all reported experiencing the same problem. While his solution was not going to sell on the mass market via Wal-Mart, he could sell it to individuals in his field and to retailers of excavating equipment. In fact, he could probably sell it at a premium price because it was a small niche market, and his invention was the only real marketed solution to that problem.

Broad Market Example

When the problem that your invention solves is experienced by a broad market, you have an opportunity for great commercial success. However, success is not guaranteed! You must invent a solution that will appeal to that broad market and be affordable.

For example, people make pancakes, hamburgers, eggs, and other foods at home that require flipping during the food preparation process. Before the spatula came along, what did they do?

Well, they probably took a fork or a knife and flipped the food items as best they could. More often than not, the pancakes and hamburgers stuck to the pan. Flipping eggs with a fork would cause the yokes to break. As you can see, while a fork or knife will do the job, it's not easy or effective.

So someone came up with the spatula. It was a simple solution, it was effective, and it was inexpensive.

That's a broad-market solution to a broad problem. Every home in America most likely has a spatula in the kitchen. No doubt you have one in yours. I know I have several in my home.

Filling a Need Example

For an example of an entertainment product that fills a need, you could go to my industry, the toy and game industry. Our products don't necessarily solve problems that perplex or trouble people. But they satisfy people's need for recreation. We all want diversion from our day-to-day activities.

Part 1 - The Inventor Mindset

We all want and need social interaction. We want to have fun with guests and family members. Games and toys satisfy that need, and they appeal to a broad market.

What games or toys will children play with? What games will adults play? And can you invent that diversion that people will enjoy for a long time?

What You Must Do

So this is what you want to do. You, like all of us, experience problems and face challenges in your day-to-day life. Now come up with a solution for one of them.

That's how inventors are born. Many inventors are not serial inventors. They simply have experienced a problem just like the rest of us. But what separates inventors is they have come up with a solution. They then think, "Well, hey, it works well for me. Maybe I should expose my solution to the world and resolve this problem for other people."

So I ask you:

- What invention do you have?
- How did you come up with it?
- Does it solve a problem effectively and efficiently?
- Was it the solution to a problem that you were experiencing?

If so, you may be on to something. Why? Because if your solution resolves the problem effectively and efficiently, and if that problem is experienced by other people either in an industry or in the general population, you may have invented a product that has potential to be commercially successful, if – and here is an important point – it can be produced at a price point that people are willing to pay.

Try to Create a Solution That Appeals to a *Big* Market

The broader the market is for your solution, the greater your chance for success, the greater your chance for real income, and the greater your chance for sustained income. What is sustained income? It is income that can go on for many years through sales and royalties.

Chapter 7 - Idea Development

When I say "market," I mean the people who experience the problem that your solution addresses and who might be receptive to buying it. Could that number be a million people? Could it be ten million people? Does it have the potential to be in every household in America and, in fact, the world? Now that's a broad market!

But keep this in mind: The broader your market, the more likely it is that others are coming up with their own solutions that will compete with yours. For instance, there are already many spatulas on the market. They may be different shapes or different sizes, but they perform the same function. If today you came up with a new spatula, what would be your chances of taking over that market, or even getting a big share of it? Very slim!

So you must ask yourself:

- Does my solution effectively and efficiently resolve the problem?
- Why would consumers who experience the problem favor my solution over the solutions that are currently available?
- Is it or can it be priced competitively?

These are questions you must ask yourself when you are involved in idea development. Your solution must be better in some way than the current solutions. What makes your solution "better"? Is it cheaper, faster, more effective, more efficient? Does it look prettier? Is it better designed? If it doesn't have an appeal greater than the appeal of current solutions, people have no reason to buy it.

"Inexpensive" Is Better

One way your solution can be "better" is if it's less expensive than the current solutions.

On rare occasions, there may be no other solution out there. However, you still want your product to be as inexpensive as possible to increase its consumer appeal.

For example, my Phase 10 line of products includes the original card game that I created in 1982 and the following variations that I have created over the years:

- Phase 10 Masters Edition: goal is to complete the phases in any order
- Phase 10 Twist: a board game version of the original game
- Phase 10 MOD: another card game, a spinoff of the original card game
- Phase 10 Dice: a dice version of the original game
- Phase 10 Kids: featuring Marvel, Sesame Street's Elmo, and other famous characters

None of these versions plays exactly the same as the original. Each is unique in some way. Obviously, when you're playing with dice, it doesn't play the same way as the card game.

By varying the "game play" among the different versions, I'm trying to appeal to different people. Dice games and card games both travel easily and each is favored by different people. The board game has a broader appeal because so many people are familiar with board games and love to play them. Board game lovers may or may not play card games and dice games. Then, of course, there are some people who have bought all the versions of the game.

Phase 10 also is available in a hand-held or electronic version, while the mobile version allows people to play on iPads, iPhones, Droid phones, Blackberry, and all the top brand mobile devices. Even Kindle. Yes, Phase 10 is now on Kindle.

While Phase 10 Kids is not currently available in the United States, it is sold widely in Europe. When it was available in the United States, we licensed action characters such as the Incredible Hulk, Spiderman, Thor, Iron Man, and all the Marvel characters. We also licensed Sesame Street's characters and featured Sesame Street's Elmo on the cover of the game box while the other Sesame Street characters were on the cards.

The original card game retails in the United States at Wal-Mart and Target, where the price fluctuates usually between $5.50 and $6. As you get into more specialty retailers or regional chains, the price increases. At Walgreens and other drug store chains, it could cost between $7 and $8.

The point here is, the price makes a big difference in the number of units we sell. More Phase 10 games are sold at Wal-Mart and Target than at any other retailer. This is due in part to the fact that they sell the game at the lowest price.

Chapter 7 - Idea Development

The original Phase 10 game is sold at a lower price than all of the other versions. Millions of the original are sold annually. The dice, kids, and other versions of the original don't sell as many units annually as the original. While one reason is that they don't have the same level of player following as the original, another is that they all are sold at higher price points.

The board game, which is my most expensive offering, retails at somewhere near $20; we sell a lot fewer of them than we do the original card game or any of the other versions.

If all I had was the board game, I would probably sell more of them than we currently do. But when people see the price of the board game and they say, "Hey, I could buy the card game for a lot less," they oftentimes choose the card game.

At the lower price of $5 to $8, it's more of an impulse item. People will think about it more as the price goes up to $20 and beyond, and they are less likely to buy it. It doesn't mean they won't. Obviously, thousands of products are sold at high price points. But, since the board game's selling price is generally two and a half times that of the original card game, we sell only about one-tenth as many. Broader appeal is garnered by having an inexpensive price point.

When You're Creating Your Invention…

Another advantage of inexpensive products is, it's easier to find licensees.

A manufacturer will more likely take a chance on your product if it can be produced inexpensively. If production will be costly, they have to really think about it because they have to expend a lot more resources to develop and market it. So licensees tend to shy away from unproven *expensive* products.

By the same token, if you decide to forego licensing and go into the venturing or manufacturing side, you can get into the business with a lot less financial resources because you are developing and producing an inexpensive product.

For example, thirty years ago, I could produce Phase 10 games for about a dollar, while I was selling them to retailers for $2.50. Not a bad margin, right? Today, due to volume, the cost is even less. My licensees are still producing them for less than a dollar and wholesaling them to retailers for a lot more than I did. They have HUGE margins!

On the other hand, if a product cost $80 to produce, you would have to sell it probably for $160, $180, or more to have a reasonable margin. Any retailer you approach will have to think carefully before spending that kind of money.

I was watching *Shark Tank* one evening. A gentleman was pitching an inexpensive solution to a pervasive problem.

A lot of people wear reading glasses. The problem is they often set them down somewhere when they aren't using them and then they can't find them, even when they put them on their heads. In the old days, people attached chains to their glasses and let them hang around their necks. I don't think I've seen those chains since high school but the problem still persists.

So this guy on *Shark Tank* created a device that was basically a little strip of metal, maybe two inches long and a quarter-inch wide. It had magnets on the back and you could clip it to your shirt. The magnets would go inside your shirt or blouse and the strip of metal would hang on the outside. It had a little U-shaped piece on it where you could hang your glasses.

When I first saw it, I thought, "Hey, this looks pretty interesting." I think he got a deal with Lori Greiner, the QVC lady. They projected that they would sell millions of these devices. They did!

Millions of reading glasses are sold throughout the world, so there was a broad market for this device. It was inexpensive to produce so they could easily test it and get it out there. People could buy it on impulse without spending a lot of money.

On the other hand, inventors with devices that cost them hundreds of dollars to make rarely get deals with the sharks. Why? Expensive products mean expensive startup costs, expensive development costs, and expensive costs in production and inventory. These products are also expensive at retail.

Sometimes the margins aren't high enough because the manufacturers don't want to run the retail price up even more with a high wholesale cost. So manufacturers try to keep their wholesale costs down, which squeezes their margins and makes it more difficult to be profitable.

Chapter 7 - Idea Development

High-Price Products

So you want to keep your product within a price point people are willing to spend for it. You can either make your product inexpensively or you can make it of such perceived fine quality and value that people will spend more than a competitive price for it.

Think of the Apple iPhone. It does basically the same thing most smart phones do, right? However, because it's Apple and it's got a great design and Apple was the first to make smart phones the way they do, people spend more money for them – a lot more money!

Don't count on this happening to you. You have a new, unproven product with no brand recognition and you are unknown as an inventor. You don't want it to be so expensive that people will shy away from it. You want it to be competitive and the best and easiest way to be competitive is to produce a product that is less expensive at retail than the competing products are.

Keep It SIMPLE!

The simpler your idea is, the simpler your solution will be, and the more likely it's going to have a broad appeal. Simple products are more likely to be inexpensive to produce as well. Also, more people will understand its purpose on site, without a lot of explanation or product demonstration. The problem it solves and why customers should buy it will be or should be evident.

By keeping it simple, you keep it consumable because people can realize instantly what problem it solves and how it is used. When you look at a spatula you see that it's flat. Someone flips a burger with it, boom. You know instantly what its purpose is. Strive to make your invention that simple.

The "WOW" Factor

In your effort to develop a product that will appeal to a large market, strive for the "wow" factor.

What I mean by this is, make your product exciting, fun, fascinating, beautiful. It should be innovative or extraordinary in some way so that when people see it they will say, "Wow, that's what I've been looking for." You will have an easier time achieving this "wow" factor when you have an entertainment-related product. People will say, "Wow, I enjoy playing that game." Or, "That toy is great for my child." Or, "That recreational activity is fun."

Part 1 - The Inventor Mindset

Think of your reaction when you first saw a smart phone demonstrated. I remember mine. When I first saw the Apple iPhone on a news channel, the presenter took her finger and swiped it over the screen and all the images went sweeping by. The apps, images, and thumbnails moved in the direction of the sweep. I thought to myself, "Wow, that's cool."

I'm pretty sure most of America had the same reaction when they saw their first Apple iPhones: "Wow, that's cool."

Not every product is going to have a "wow" factor. If you can come up with one that does, you've got a good shot at success.

Good Profit Margin

Previously, I talked about creating products that have good profit margins. Profit margin is the difference between the cost to produce, package, and distribute a product, and the price charged for it.

If, for instance, your product is created by your own company as a venture or through a license deal with a manufacturer, and it costs you $5 to manufacture and then you sell it wholesale to retailers like Wal-Mart or Target at $10, your profit margin is 50%.

Typically you want to have *at least a 50% profit margin*. More, of course, is better. From that 50% margin, you've got to cover all of your "overhead" costs, those "fixed" costs associated with running your business, including your office and your non-production employees, like your secretary and your bookkeeper.

Many licensees will not bring a product to market unless they can get a 50% margin. If you watch *Shark Tank*, you've probably noticed the first questions the sharks ask the business owners are about margin:

- "What does it cost you to make it?"
- "What do you sell it for?"

The sharks are trying to figure out the profit margin because they know that if you don't have at least a 50% profit margin you are less likely to be profitable. And, of course, they're in it for the money. So are your potential licensees and manufacturers. You should be, too!

Chapter 7 - Idea Development

Common Materials and Technologies

Another valuable way to keep your costs down is to come up with a product that uses common materials and existing technologies in its production.

Even if your product is so revolutionary, so innovative, that it blows everyone away, if you require uncommon materials and advanced technology to produce it, it will be costly. Licensees will hesitate to make the investment needed to produce it. Investors will be reluctant to help you fund your venture. I'm not saying an advanced product is impossible to develop, only that you will have a more difficult time securing support for it because of its cost to develop.

Will People "Pay" the Price?

One of the most important questions you must answer is, "Will people pay the price of my invention?" Without the answer, you could find out too late that no one is willing to buy it at the price you require to make a profit.

Let me give you an example. I met an inventor who came up with an "in-garage" car wash. It was a great idea. In fact, the way I came across the idea was as a consumer planning to buy my wife a new car.

One evening, while we were talking about what we wanted in a new car, she mentioned that she was troubled by how hard it is to keep a car clean. We live in Michigan, by the way, and the winters are ... well, they can be pretty severe. Metropolitan Detroit sets atop a 1,500-acre salt mine so salt is used heavily across Michigan throughout most of the winter and it is harsh on cars. "Who wants a new car that looks like it's been driven through a dirt and grime factory?" she asked.

I said, "Wouldn't it be great if you could wash your car every day at home without the hassle and time required to do so yourself?"

The next day, I happened to be reading an online news magazine and I saw an article about a gentleman named Dale who had created an in-your-own-garage car wash system. I was fascinated. The article didn't get into a whole lot of detail, but it told enough that I thought, "Hey, this is interesting. Let me check it out."

So I did a Google search of the company name, got Dale's phone number, and gave him a call. He happened to be in Scottsdale, Arizona, where I had once lived, so we had an interesting conversation about Scottsdale.

Then we got into talking about his product and its basic function. He said the whole apparatus fit into a standard garage and didn't require any more space than the size of a vehicle. It extended slightly a foot or two around the sides of the vehicle.

You drive your car into the garage and up the small platform and then a Mylar curtain comes down, completely surrounding the vehicle and forming a watertight seal around the platform. Several water jets begin spraying your vehicle, first with water and then with soap, much like you see in a car wash.

After spraying soap for a few minutes, the jets once again spray water on the vehicle until the soap has rinsed away. No brushes are used. The intensity of the spraying, both water and soap, is enough to clean the average vehicle under average conditions. Cars that are super grimy and dirty may, he said, require a couple of washes.

After the last rinse, a dryer, basically a built-in furnace, comes on. The dryer vents open up and blow air on the vehicle, and this is how the car is dried.

This whole operation may take up to four hours. So, at the end of the day, you drive the car onto the platform. As you're going into your house, you simply push the button on the control panel on the wall to start the wash. By the next morning, when you open the garage door, you find the curtain up on the platform and your car is showroom clean. I'm thinking, "Great idea! I have a problem; he has a solution."

Then I said, "Okay, what does this thing cost?" Now I knew, after reading about it in the magazine, and watching the video of the car wash in action, and hearing him tell me all about its features, that this was not going to be cheap. But I could see, from the video of the system in action, it seemed to work beautifully and did a great job. I was ready to buy.

"Twenty-nine thousand dollars," he said, "plus, $5,000 installation fee." I was looking at 34,000 bucks. I told him I wasn't interested. For $10,000 or $15,000, I would have bought it. But at $34,000, no way!

I asked friends, who I knew could afford to pay the price if they wanted, what they thought. They were investors as well. One owned several businesses including a bank. Another was a respected doctor in the area.

They agreed that being able to get your car washed in your garage while having dinner in your kitchen was a good idea, and if it cost $5,000, or $10,000, or even $15,000 they might buy it. But $34,000 was too high. Just because you have a lot of money doesn't mean you're going to overpay for a product whose cost far outweighs its benefit.

Personally, I'll continue to take my car to the neighborhood car wash and spend the $5 or $10 to sit inside my car for fifteen minutes and watch my car get washed.

My point in telling you this story is to let you know that, when you are creating a product, you want it to have a price point that people are willing to pay. As part of the research evaluation, step 1 of *The Simple Plan*, you must determine the public's willingness to pay the price you require.

As you're building the product, look at the materials, the effort, and the labor that are needed. Figure out what it all will cost, which is your wholesale cost, and then what you will have to charge a retailer to recoup your expenses and make a profit. Look at the other solutions in the marketplace and determine if the retail price of your invention/product is competitive with theirs.

Dale told me only one other company built an in-your-garage car wash system. While it actually functioned quite differently from his, it, too, was expensive but it had found a market in brand new homes and as part of the new-build process.

Dale's system was an "aftermarket" solution. It went into garages that were already built. To date, to my knowledge, he has not sold one, even after several years, even in Scottsdale, where a lot of people could afford to buy it if they wanted it.

If you want your product to sell at retail at an inexpensive price point, you have to make sure it *can be produced at an inexpensive price point.* That means you need to look carefully at what you are paying for materials, labor, and technology. If they are too high, your retail price will be too high as well, and people won't spend the money.

Study the Market and Marketplace

Finally, you need to study your market and the marketplace. The "market" refers to the potential consumers of your product. The "marketplace" includes the distribution channels of the product. If you've got a new spatula, you need to study the kitchen and housewares market. Observe the behavior and the cooking habits of people to make sure that it has utility for them. Determine that it will be effective and efficient and that it can be produced at a price people are willing to pay.

Make certain that your product resolves a real problem that enough people have to enable you to obtain a share of the market from your competitors or create a new market.

And if it doesn't, if all signs are telling you that it will not work, let it go and move on to your next idea.

Some ideas or inventions are just fads. They're not meant to last for decades or even years. They're just not going to be in the marketplace for a long time. That's okay! If your product lasts even one season, you still can make good money from it.

Remember the pet rock? There was no way it was going to be a long-term success. But it was a great success for a short period of time. Millions were sold. The same thing could happen to you. Your product could have a short lifespan but earn you good money, maybe even millions of dollars that you could invest in other inventions, or put away for your kids' college tuition, or splurge on some of life's luxuries, whatever that means to you.

So continue to think and to evaluate your ideas. Be persistent. Don't give in easily to discouragement. Watch out for warning signs and stop when they say stop. Otherwise, go forward.

Remember, your vision and creativity can bring a product into the world that enhances people's lives, brings them joy and satisfaction, resolves their problems, and makes their lives easier. That's an occupational benefit that only inventors can enjoy.

Part 2:

The Simple Plan

Chapter 8

Step 1 of The Simple Plan:

Research Evaluation

"The major difference between the big shot and the little shot is the big shot is just a little shot who kept on shooting." Zig Ziglar

"Don't wait for your ship to come in; swim out to it." Cathy Hopkins

I wish I could help every one of you come up with ideas that were marketable and could bring you success, but that's not what this book is about. This book presumes that you already have an idea in mind, or have already created an invention.

In part 1 of this book, I helped you establish the inventor's mindset to enable you to develop your idea and bring it into the world. What do you do now? How do you bring it into the world successfully? You follow the six easy steps of *The Simple Plan*:

1. Research Evaluation
2. Prototype Development
3. Product Evaluation
4. Provisional Patent Application
5. Intellectual Property Registration
6. License/Venture

In this chapter, we focus on step one: Research Evaluation.

Your Idea Is the Easy Part

Thomas Edison, who is arguably the most renowned inventor of all time, once said, "Genius is 1% inspiration and 99% perspiration."

That's an interesting thought. Our ingenious idea is 1% of the process.

Part 2 - The Simple Plan

The hard work of getting that idea into the marketplace comes after you've come up with the idea. I always tell inventors, "Look, the easiest part of the process is creating the concept in your head. The real work is separating the likely commercial successes from the likely commercial failures by determining which have the best chances of making it from idea in your head to item on the store shelf."

Most new inventors are puzzled when I share that revelation. They think it was hard enough coming up with their good ideas. I believe coming up with good ideas is not difficult. A truly good idea is born from a problem. If you come up with a tool that alleviates that problem, you have created a solution that others who experience the same problem may find interesting. The idea is developed as a solution to that need.

You and Everyone Else

If you have a marketable idea, you are like everyone else on the planet who has made it to adulthood. Why do I say this? Because we all have needs. Issues and problems fill our lives and require solutions. If the market already offers us solutions, we use them. If not, we come up with our own ideas. What separates inventors from everyone else? Inventors take action on our ideas.

As an inventor, you probably have many invention ideas in your head. Not all of your ideas have the potential of being commercial successes. But one probably does.

How do you determine which idea that is? How do you prioritize your many ideas so that you focus on bringing the ones with the most potential to the marketplace first?

And how do you find out if your idea is already in the marketplace, hidden in some remote corner of the industry that isn't readily apparent to you?

Making that determination is part of what you do during the research evaluation, which is step one of my simple plan.

During a research evaluation you find answers to questions such as:

- Is my idea already out there?
- Is it truly a new idea?
- Does it have commercial possibilities?

Chapter 8 - Step 1 of The Simple Plan: Research Evaluation

The Simple Plan takes you step by step through the process of:

- creating a tangible form out of a concept in your head, then either

- getting it into the marketplace through a license or venture deal, or

- determining that your idea will not likely have commercial success and moving on to your next idea.

Thomas Edison had it right. He created many inventions, and he failed at many, often many times in the process. Most of yours may fail as well, and for so many different reasons:

- The market isn't ready for it.

- There isn't a big enough need.

- It can't be produced at a price that people are willing to pay.

- Technology has to advance more so that you can lower your price.

Let them go. Devote your effort to pursuing your gems – after you use *The Simple Plan* to figure out which ones are the gems.

Why Inventions Fail

The research evaluation will help you separate your gems from your garbage. By eliminating inventions that fail the evaluation, you can stop wasting time and money on bad ideas and move on to your potentially good ideas. By determining the market and marketability of your invention you can find your invention gems.

Most inventions never become successful despite all of the valid arguments that could be made for their practicality, usefulness, and genius. How can I make that statement? It's simple.

Most inventions fail for one or more of the following reasons:

- The product is ahead of its time.

- The inventor didn't act upon the opportunity it presented.

- The inventor didn't devote the right resources to getting it into the marketplace.

- The inventor never developed a sound prototype to demonstrate how the concept resolved the problem.

- There is no market for the invention or the market rejects it.

- The competition is too strong and entrenched.

As an independent inventor, your competition is larger than you might believe even if you already believe it's large.

My industry, the game industry, may be one of the most competitive industries on the planet. Thousands of new games are invented every year. You, too, will face competition within the industry of your invention whatever it is. However, a well-done research evaluation will increase your likelihood of success.

Needless to say, inventing is an uncertain process at times. Sometimes we think we have a winner and then we evaluate it and determine it's not what we thought it was.

Therefore, I encourage inventors to avoid spending much money, particularly developing prototypes or patents, until they've done at least a research evaluation. We'll get into the forms of research later. For now, conserve your cash as much as possible until your evaluation is complete. Otherwise, you could end up spending a lot of money developing an idea that is going nowhere.

I made the mistake of not evaluating the potential of my first game, Dice Baseball. I was 19 when I first started trying to launch it into the market. I didn't ask anyone for their opinions of the game or their evaluations of the product. I didn't play it with any focus groups. I just launched it. And it failed. It wasn't acceptable to the market for a number of reasons.

Had I done a proper research evaluation, I would have saved myself a lot of time and money.

Chapter 8 - Step 1 of The Simple Plan: Research Evaluation

What Is a Profitably Marketable Invention?

At its most basic level, a profitably marketable invention is

(A) great idea

(B A solution to a problem or fulfillment of a need

(C) Both of the above

(D) Neither of the above

If you guessed B, you're right.

A great invention is a solution to a problem that is present among consumers in the marketplace. Not every "great idea" solves a problem, and if it doesn't solve a problem or fill a need, people won't buy it.

A "great idea" may not necessarily have a great marketable chance of success.

Ask yourself these questions:

• *What is the problem I'm trying to solve with my invention?*

You probably came up with your invention idea as a resolution to a problem. How well does your invention solve the problem? If it does satisfactorily, then you're on the right track.

Now take your solution into the real world, because you can't adequately evaluate your invention while sitting in your armchair. Look at as many situations as possible where the problem is likely to occur. Are other people experiencing the same problem?

• *How does your product compare to your competitors?*

If other people are experiencing the same problem, what solutions are they using?

How well does your invention resolve the problem compared to competing products or solutions?

• *Is your solution more complex to manufacture than the competition?*

Part 2 - The Simple Plan

Some inventions cannot be produced at a profitable price. Others are so advanced that there is no current manufacturing process available. Maybe the materials needed for its manufacturing are too expensive or scarce, which may result in high production cost.

If your solution is complex to manufacture for any of these or other reasons, you may have to ask a higher retail price. Is your solution superior enough to your competition to justify the higher price? Will consumers pay it?

• Is your solution more complex to use than the competition?

If so, will consumers take the extra time needed to learn how to operate it?

• *Are the benefits of your product easily identified?*

Can a person look at it or take a second to use it and easily determine how it will resolve their problem?

• *Is your invention more or less likely than the competition to cause accidental injury to a user?*

Obviously you don't want to create a hazardous product, but you'd be surprised how many new inventions that seem beneficial actually can cause injury. If yours is one of them, your liability concerns will increase, as will the liability insurance coverage needed by you and the manufacturer.

• *Can your invention list as many benefits on its packaging as your competition?*

Are they the same benefits or different ones? How will your product resolve the problem for the consumer? Can the benefits be described in just a few words?

• *What is your product's environmental impact?*

Increasingly, people are becoming green. When they shop, they look for environmentally friendly products and solutions. In response to this evolving change in consciousness, governments and businesses the world over are moving away from fossil fuels and getting more deeply into renewables.

Your product, when it is being manufactured in the factory and when it is being used by the consumer, must not pose a hazard or be a detriment to the environment. It must not increase pollution. If your business doesn't keep up with the times, you are creating an unnecessary obstacle in the way of your success.

When to STOP the Inventing Process

You'll want to stop the inventing process if you determine that:

• *Your product already exists on the market.*

If your product, in its exact form, with the same benefits and the same features, is already in the marketplace, you need to stop and take a hard look at what you are doing. Why would people stop buying brand X and start buying your product?

You have to be honest and objective. Can you sell it for a lower price? Is it easier to operate?

If you say, "Well, this is no problem at all," knowing deep down inside that it is, you're cheating yourself and wasting your time and money.

• *You find a better product than yours on the market.*

Obviously you need to stop, okay? Don't waste your time or money if there's a better solution. Why would people go from brand X, which is a better product, and start buying your inferior product? Your product must be better in some way. Better could be higher quality, lower price, added benefits, unique features, stronger materials, healthier ingredients, ease of use, efficiency, or effectiveness.

• *You find multiple products similar to yours already on the market and priced comparably to yours.*

You'll want to stop the inventing process if while doing your due diligence you find three or four solutions out there that are about the same as yours, no better, no worse. Again, why would people stop buying brand X, Y, and Z that have been on the market long enough to be ingrained in consumers' lifestyles and habits? You might say yours is cheaper, but is it really? We'll talk about that later in this chapter.

• *Your solution works less than 99% of the time in solving the problem.*

Actually that number is low. Ideally your solution should work 100% of the time, but you can be forgiven for not being perfect. In fact, there might be certain situations where 99% is good enough.

For example, some medications may be FDA-approved and considered to be "safe and effective" yet may not provide a cure or relief in every case and for everyone. On the other hand, if you have invented a consumer or industrial product that you know only works "most of the time," it's ridiculous to work on it. Why would people buy it? They likely would not.

> • *You are unwilling to honestly evaluate your invention against competing solutions.*

You're setting yourself up for failure. Do yourself a favor and stop immediately.

Friends and Family Evaluation

Now we're going to focus on several ways you can evaluate consumer responses to your invention. The first one is the friends and family evaluation. I like this one because it costs you nothing or next to nothing, but beware of the drawbacks.

The number one drawback is this: Most friends and family are not qualified or objective enough to give a meaningful evaluation. They love you. They don't want to hurt your feelings and dampen your enthusiasm. Many of them would rather lie to you than to hurt your feeling. So most are going to tell you your invention is the greatest invention since sliced bread. They may feel genuinely hopeful about it. However, most of them, maybe even all of them, are not technical or marketing experts in the field of your invention; and personally they're all too close to you.

Having said all the above, I still think friends and family can and should be the first people you ask about your invention. Just know that, while their feedback may give you a warm and fuzzy feeling and some motivation, *you cannot solely rely on it*. So if you still decide to ask your friends and family for their opinions, be ready with follow-up questions to their initial answers. Push them to be specific, to drill down, to help you to determine their true feelings.

If they say they "dislike the idea," ask them why. Is the price too high? Is the design faulty? Is it ineffective in doing what you said it would do? Does another product do it better?

If they say they "like the idea," ask them what they like about it. How is it superior to other products on the market?

Do they have another solution that they use and like better? What's better about it?

If they say they would buy it, ask them how much they would spend for it.

If you are reading this book after having produced your invention, your garage may already be overflowing with your product. If that's the case, ask them if they would purchase one from you. In this way you will test their desire to have one and help you determine whether they really like it. Your goal here is not to sell one but rather to find out what they really think.

Most important, don't just accept "I like it" or "I don't like it." Find out why and what you can do to make it better. Trust your friends and family for what they do best: provide you encouragement and support with honesty.

However, never solely trust the *opinions* of friends or relatives about the future success of your invention, because, *unless they are technical or marketing experts in the field of your invention*, they don't know.

I'm not saying they're bad people for guessing or for lying out of love. I'm just saying that, because they don't have the expertise in the field, you cannot proceed to spend tens of thousands of dollars based solely on their opinion. But they are a good place to begin your research evaluation.

Thank your friends and family for their views whether they are positive or negative. Then move on to your next form of evaluation.

3 Core Elements You *Must* Research

The research evaluation has three key elements:

- Market research
- Competition research
- Patentability research

Market Research

Market research is the analytical stage where you determine the overall

95

market for your invention, or if there is no market at all. If there is a market, how big is it?

For instance, if you've created a new car seat device for infants traveling in automobiles, you will want to determine how many car seats are sold in the country and around the world every year. What is the average price of those car seats, and the price range, from least expensive to most expensive? How does the quality differ as the price increases?

Is the market trending upward or downward? For example, if last year 10 million infant car seats were sold, did they sell 5 million in the previous year or did they sell 15 million? Knowing if the trend is upward or downward will guide your decision on whether or not to enter that particular space and what your offering should be if you decide to go forward.

Do you need to add more value or more features to your car seat so that it can buck the trend or beat out the competition?

Market research will give you answers to these questions.

What I've learned after forty-plus years as an inventor is this: Market research is absolutely hands down the *most critical step in the inventing process.* It doesn't matter how great your prototype is. It doesn't matter how strong your patent is. It doesn't matter how great you are at business and how big a company you think you can develop around this product. None of that matters if you haven't properly evaluated your invention's market potential.

That's why market research is the first part of the overall research evaluation.

Market research consists of two sections:

- Primary research
- Secondary research

Primary Research

Primary research provides firsthand information generated from research actions you've taken directly. This might include surveys, questionnaires, interviews, and any other methods of gathering original data.

Chapter 8 - Step 1 of The Simple Plan: Research Evaluation

It could be extensive and detailed, such as a survey of 1,000 potential customers. Or it may be as simple as interviewing a small cross-section of potential customers. (In my view, the more people you interview or survey, the better.)

Primary market research is often customer focused. When it is, your objective is to find out who the customers are for your product.

- Where are they located?
- Where do you find them?
- How do you target them?
- Why will they buy your product?
- What problem does it solve for them?
- Why would they buy your product over competing products?
- How unique is your product to the consumer?
- What unique benefits does it offer?

If you have identified a problem that few other people encounter, there likely will be little competition. That could mean that the problem isn't large enough to merit production of a resolution, which means there's no need for your solution. It may be time to let it go.

But if you have identified a problem that is encountered by a large number of people, then there probably is competition. You need to determine how your product's benefits outweigh those of the competition.

- Why will the consumer want the benefits offered by your invention?
- Will the consumer pay more or less than the competition for your product?
- Will there be a foreign market?

If your product relates to human beings, along with the domestic market, you probably should look at the foreign market as well because human beings share so many problems regardless of country, race, religion, or ethnicity.

97

Secondary Research

Secondary research is data you accumulate from other sources. When you look up statistical surveys or information on your invention or its industry at the library or run a comprehensive article search online, the information you gather is secondary research. Other people or companies have done the studies or interviews for their own purposes. You can apply the results to your invention or business.

Finding valuable secondary research can save you a lot of time and money. It can give you demographic data, national sales figures, and specific competitors.

You'll seek answers to questions such as:

- What is your industry's history?
- Is it growing or declining?
- Who are the key players and what are their annual sales?
- What are the barriers of entry into your industry, if any?
- How large is the market for your invention? What government regulations, if any, relate to your product and industry and what are their effects?

You'll learn about trade associations related to your industry and join some of them.

You'll discover the trade shows associated with your invention's industry and attend some of them.

You'll find the industry and trade publications that are out there and subscribe to some of them.

Through all of these sources of information, you will discover a wealth of knowledge and experience. The trade association has answers to many of your data-driven questions. The industry publications will introduce you to the key players in the industry and give you insight into what your competition is doing.

At trade shows, you can actually walk the aisles, meet your competitors, see their products, even demo them, and then compare their benefits and features to yours.

Chapter 8 - Step 1 of The Simple Plan: Research Evaluation

Through secondary research, you will learn to spot trends in your industry concerning your customers, your competition, and the industry in general.

When I first started in the toy industry, I went to the New York Toy Fair, which is held annually in February in New York City. By going to Toy Fair, I could see the other products that were being offered before they were widely introduced to the market.

Among the new games I saw at Toy Fair were Balderdash, Greed, and Jenga.

Toys I saw included Teddy Ruxpin, Furbies, and Rubik's Cube.

I met industry people who later helped me with Phase 10. Some were suppliers and others were game manufacturers and representatives.

I met people from Carta Mundi, the Belgian firm that later I used to make the card decks for Phase 10. They continue to make the Phase 10 card decks for Mattel today.

While I never set up a booth at Toy Fair, I walked the floor and met many people and made great connections.

You can do likewise. Talk to long-time attendees and first-timers. Ask them how they're doing and how their companies are doing. What trends do they see, including in distribution, and what are they doing in response? Make contact with people and companies that could provide services to you and your invention.

Competition Research

The second core element of research evaluation is the competition research. Who are your competitors? How entrenched are they in the market? What are their respective market shares?

How is market share distributed among competitors? For instance, if there are five competitors, does one control 80% of the market and the other four divide up the remaining 20%? Or do they each have roughly 20%, a more diverse spread of the market share?

What are the competing products? Look at each one and determine how it resolves the main problem that your product resolves. How effective and efficient are they? How do their prices compare with the price you have in mind for your solution?

Part 2 - The Simple Plan

You'll research the following:

- What are the features and benefits of the competing products?
- How do those features and benefits relate to your product?
- Who are the major direct competitors?

In my industry, major competitors are other game manufacturing companies, and, more specifically, card game manufacturing companies. My game is licensed to Mattel. Mattel also distributes the card games Uno and Skip-Bo, respectively the number one and number three best-selling card games. So while they are competition to me in the card game space, all three are manufactured by the same company. Card games that are manufactured by other companies are direct competitors as well.

In your case, how do the competition's products compare with yours? What are their sales? If the manufacturer is a public company, look at their annual reports and their quarterly reports.

You won't find this information so easily for private companies. Nevertheless, a valuable source of information can be buyers or retailers. Ask them, "How does Brand X sell compared to Brand Z? People will often tell you what you need to know if you just ask.

In addition to associates of a public company, you can talk to industry insiders. They can give you insight into sales, names of the big competitors, their respective market shares, and often-valuable general "guesses."

And what if there is no direct competition in your invention's space?

Some see that as a great benefit. I often hear inventors say, "No one else is selling this kind of product. I've got it made." This is good news to you if you have opened up a new market and your product is the first. But, a I said earlier, the fact that there is no competition may also mean that there's no market for your invention. Which is the case for you?

In review, if your invention solves a problem (it must – or you're in big trouble!), you need to find out what product people are using now to solve that problem. Ask your friends and family. Talk about it in focus groups. Examine:

- How much did they pay for it?
- How is it made?

• How did they discover it on the market?

• What do they like and dislike about it?

And any other questions you can think of about the competing products.

Through these methods of primary and secondary research and competition research, you will gain indispensable insight into your industry and your competition. You can approach your next steps with the understanding of what's in front of you.

Patentability Research

The third step of the research evaluation is patentability research. You may be thinking, "Ken, I'm not interested in patenting my invention." You may consider it more appropriate to register your copyright or trademark. Or you may think it better to maintain a trade secret.

Whether or not you intend to apply for a patent, it is wise to do patentability research for two reasons:

• First, and most important, you want to make sure that your invention does not infringe on someone else's patent.

• Second, if you want to eventually apply for a patent on your invention, the patent research will give you an initial idea of whether or not you can potentially apply for one.

If you do the preliminary patent research yourself, your only cost is your time if you go on the Internet and search on these two sites:

• Google Patents: https://patents.google.com

• United States Patent and Trade Office: www.uspto.gov

Use keywords associated with your invention. For instance, if I were doing a patentability search on a card game, I would punch in "card game," "games," "cards," "rummy card games," and other keywords and phrases associated with card games and the method of playing the game to find all of the patents related to those keywords. Reading the general descriptions of the patents found as a result of the search would inform me on how close they are to my game.

Part 2 - The Simple Plan

If you don't want to do the search yourself, you can hire a patent agent or attorney or a patent search firm and, for a few hundred dollars, they will do a patentability examination for you. For that low amount, the search may not be absolutely thorough. But you will gain enough information to know if you're likely infringing on someone else's patent, which is the main reason for this third part of the research evaluation.

Patentability research is subjective and depends primarily on the skill of the searcher, the interpretation of the results, and the money that you're willing to spend to conduct the patent search. Whether you do the basic search yourself or hire a patent research specialist to do the research for you, doing a patent evaluation will give you a feel for what solutions are out there that compete with your invention. From there you can determine if your invention is patentable. If it's not patentable for some reason, you can approach it with that understanding. If it is possibly patentable, you can apply for the patent when that time comes or forego a patent if that makes sense.

However, keep in mind, regardless of how you do the search, and regardless of the outcome, that now is *not* the time in *The Simple Plan* to seek a patent. That comes later, in step five, which I'll talk about in chapter 12. Right now you just want to avoid infringing on someone else's patent and get a general idea of your idea's potential patentability.

How to Talk about Your Idea without Revealing It

You can ask questions and talk to people about your concept without telling them what your invention is. How do you do that? I'm asked this question often when I speak to inventor groups.

It's simple: You discuss the *problem* and you discuss the *benefits* of your invention without discussing *how* your invention does what it does. How it does what it does is the patentable secret. The fact that it does it is not. So if your invention detangles hair better than anyone else's comb, you may ask:

- Do you ever have problems detangling your hair?

- How do you resolve that problem now?

- If there was a product that could detangle your hair faster and better than what you're doing now, what would you pay for such a solution?

102

Chapter 8 - Step 1 of The Simple Plan: Research Evaluation

These questions provide you with valuable information without your having to reveal the mechanics of your solution, or the "secret sauce" of how your invention solves the problem.

This style of questioning does not reveal how your comb detangles hair better than other combs. This is the kind of approach you should take if you have not received or requested a signed non-disclosure agreement (NDA) from them, as we discussed in chapter 4.

Independent Evaluation Sources

Another way to evaluate the marketability and commercial feasibility of your invention is by using the Preliminary Innovation Evaluation System (PIES), which was developed some years ago by a gentleman named Dr. Udell.

PIES attempts to look at between thirty and forty of the most important characteristics a new product should have and then it ranks each with a score of 0 to 100, where 0 means that it will definitely NOT be successful and 100 means it WILL definitely be successful. PIES is one of the better evaluation formats out there today; all of the most critical aspects of launching an invention are evaluated through it.

PIES can be helpful in the same way that a business plan can be helpful to an entrepreneur. It gives you a guidepost to follow as you move forward. If you use it correctly with input from experts in your industry, you will be forced to look objectively at your invention from all angles and think about aspects of it that you may have overlooked.

The following are three well-known, reputable organizations that offer PIES or similar marketability evaluations. If you have the funds, I recommend that you have two or three done for comparison purposes. You may pick up insight from one that is lacking in another. Their prices can range anywhere from $300 to $995.

Wisconsin Innovation Services Center

University of Wisconsin, Whitewater

1200 Hyland 800

Whitewater, WI 53190

262-472-1365

Part 2 - The Simple Plan

http://www.wisconsinsbdc.org/wisc

Tekcapital, LLC

Invention Evaluator

12000 Biscayne Blvd.

Suite 222

North Miami, FL. 33181

305-200-3450

http://www.inventionevaluator.com

Inventicator

Invention City

P. O. Box 493

East Orleans, MA 02643

612-808-8081

http://www.inventioncity.com/inventicator

Other evaluation resources that are out there will not cost you any money. But if you can afford it, these are worthwhile resources. They will keep your invention confidential. They don't steal ideas. They work hard to help you determine the marketability of your invention. And they will have an answer for you in a matter of weeks. Inventors I've known who have gone through the process reported that they received objective viewpoints and thorough evaluations, and that the benefits were worth the expense.

Conclusion

Research is the most critical step of the inventing process. It doesn't matter if you can patent your invention. It doesn't matter whether you can make a prototype of it. If you don't have a product that has potential for commercial success, you're wasting your time. The only way to get some idea of that potential is to do a research evaluation in the ways we've just discussed.

Chapter 8 - Step 1 of The Simple Plan: Research Evaluation

You can go through the key elements listed in this chapter. Not all will apply to your invention, but many will.

You'll do a brief *friends and family* evaluation by asking them key questions about your invention and finding out their general opinions. While it's not to be relied upon as the definitive answer to your invention's commercial potential, it's an easy first step.

Then you'll move on and either:

- Do the research yourself using the three core elements: market research, competition research, and patentability research. Or,

- Do a PIES evaluation: Go to one or more of the three institutions I introduced you to and get each to do an objective evaluation for you. For a cost of between $300 and $995, each one is a worthwhile investment.

Regardless of how you do it, you must do an honest, objective research evaluation because it means the difference between success and failure. By skipping the research and running straight to market or to the patent office, or to creating a prototype, you could be wasting tens of thousands of dollars and hours of your time that you will never get back.

Remember, over 90% of all patents issued by the U.S. Patent Office do not yield enough money to recover the cost of the patent. In other words, the person applying for the patent has wasted time and money.

Don't let that person be you!

Chapter 9

Step 2 of The Simple Plan:

Prototype Development

"Whether you think you can or think you can't, you're right!"
Henry Ford

"The only limit to our realization of tomorrow
will be our doubts of today."
Franklin D. Roosevelt

If you've done a thorough research evaluation and if the results of your evaluation encourage you to move forward, creating a prototype version of your product is your second step. You can either build it yourself or have someone build it for you. The bottom line is, you need it. In this chapter, we'll look at the reasons why and various forms and methods you can use for its construction.

You may say, "Well, Ken, wouldn't it be more reasonable to get a patent first before I build the prototype?" I say, "No, build a prototype first."

The reason I say this is because you don't know if your invention will *do* what you think it will do. You don't know if it will function properly. You don't know if it will be effective in resolving the issue you built it to resolve.

Remember, up to this point, you've taken an idea that was in your head and, by your research evaluation, tested its potential against an actual marketplace. Based on your primary and secondary research, you've determined that your *idea* can be a successful commercial product.

But can the real thing, in the form of a prototype?

Having a prototype will ensure you that your idea is effective and efficient in solving the problem and that *the concept works*.

107

Part 2 - The Simple Plan

Except for only a tiny percentage of instances when applying for a patent first makes sense, building the prototype is the step that follows the research evaluation. Applying for the patent comes later.

One reason is because your patent application should include all of the claims that you need the patent to fully protect. As experience from just about everyone has demonstrated, when you build a prototype you will find that it doesn't function as you thought it would so you will have to tweak it here and there, which means that now your patent application may no longer cover all aspects of the final invention. Or you will find that it isn't as effective or as efficient as you thought it would be; or it can't be built at a price that people will pay. There are other reasons as well why building a prototype comes first.

But, as I just noted, there are times when the opposite is true and it makes more sense to apply for your patent before you build the prototype. One of those times might be when you determine that, because of the complexity of the equipment, the cost to build the prototype is far greater than the price of the patent. In a case like that, you might apply for the patent first, cover as many claims and potential claims as you can in that application, and then build the prototype.

Prototypes of inventions that have a lot of moving parts and complexity are also expensive to build. If the cost of your prototype is projected to be $30,000, or $40,000, or $50,000, you may want to consider applying first for a patent, which probably will cost between $5,000 and $15,000.

This is especially true if your invention is a high-tech piece of equipment that you want to "protect" before you start building the prototype.

However, the vast majority of you will want to build a prototype first. Of course, *anyone* who is involved in helping you build the prototype should be required to sign a non-disclosure agreement, as we discussed in chapter 4.

Building Your Prototype

The beauty of living and inventing now, in the age of 3D printing, is that you can build prototypes for a few hundred dollars. I'm talking nice, good-looking prototypes.

You can begin by visiting your local "maker space" group. A maker space consists of a group of inventors who have collectively purchased various pieces of equipment used in developing prototypes. These might include lathes, laser cutters for metals, sewing machines, 3D printers, Cad software, and computers. Individual inventors can sign up for membership in the group and, on a "do-it-yourself" basis, have access to the equipment for the development and building of their prototypes. Many of the maker spaces also provide training on the equipment.

Some inventor clubs or groups own the 3D printers that you will need to make a good prototype with moving parts. In chapter 3, I gave you reasons why you should become associated with an inventor club. This is another one. If you're not already associated with an inventor club, I encourage you to look for one in your area and become associated with them. They'll be able to give you a lot of information about building prototypes, including where you can get them made locally.

Or you can cobble together a functioning model of a prototype from parts of other products that are already on the market. Your prototype doesn't have to look exactly how you want the final product to look. Its main purpose is to make sure the final product will *function* correctly; will solve the problem effectively and efficiently; and can be built and sold at a price point that people will pay.

It's true that there are companies that will license your idea without a prototype. However, in most cases, the inventions involved in these types of deals are extremely simple products that are inexpensive to build. By looking at a drawing or a sketch of one of these very simple products, the potential licensee can easily see its functionality and that it can do what it was designed to do.

So, Why Build a Prototype?

As can be seen, there are instances where you can license your product without building a prototype. However, in 95% of the cases, this is not going to happen. If you're serious about wanting to sell your invention or get a license deal, you're going to have to build at least a basic, rough prototype that demonstrates your product's functionality.

• *To ensure that your invention actually will work*

It's funny how many times I've actually seen people create inventions, sketch them out, do elaborate drawings, apply for patents, and spend thousands of dollars before they've ever built a prototype. Then, when they finally build their prototype, they discover that the invention doesn't work.

Or even if it works, it doesn't function effectively or efficiently and so becomes unusable, unreliable, and unwanted by the public and, therefore, completely unmarketable. So the number one reason for building a prototype is to "prove the concept," to make certain that it actually works well.

Of course, that should make sense to every one of us, right? Unfortunately, it doesn't. Don't be one of those inventors who forego the opportunity to build a prototype and test your concept. Don't let others tell you it's not necessary. Except for those few instances where production of the prototype is extremely involved, complicated, or expensive, it is a necessary second step in the inventing process, the second step of *The Simple Plan*.

• *To work out the kinks in the invention's operation*

Even if your invention works, that idea that came out of your head can probably be improved now that you're looking at a concrete form of it. Is it effective and efficient? Does it function smoothly and easily? Is it easy to learn how to use and operate?

Often, only after the prototype is built does the inventor discover problems in the design or kinks in the functionality that must be worked out.

If you apply for the patent before you build a prototype, and in the patent application you make all kinds of claims and drawings as to its functionality and form, and then you build a prototype and discover, "Wait a minute. I can't use a rubber band here; I've got to use a spring. I can't put a hole here, I have to do something else," then you have to revise your whole patent application to account for the changes that you made. This is why you build the prototype before you apply for the patent.

• *To have something tangible to show potential investors and customers*

So you want to attract angel investors, or sell stock, or bring on partners, or find store sales managers who will put your product on their shelves. In any of these instances, they probably are going to want to see the functionality and form of your invention before they act. In this way, they can see it in action and gain the necessary confidence that it actually works and does the job well.

When I was trying to bring Phase 10 to market, I built a prototype. That prototype landed me my first major customers, Kmart, the largest retailer in the country at that time, and Meijer, a growing regional chain of stores. I got purchase orders from them *before* I ever went into production.

- *To give you an idea of the invention's cost to manufacture*

Even if you say, "I'm going to get a licensee; I don't need to build a prototype and figure out manufacturing costs," you do. Here's why:

Your potential licensee will want to know. They will do their homework and eventually figure out costs on their own. But they will look to you for answers in your initial meeting with them. A knowledgeable answer, with price quotes to show how you arrived at it, can move you closer to a licensing deal. Your potential licensee will now be able to determine what the retail price will be and if people will pay it. Not having a knowledgeable answer can derail the licensing process.

Building a prototype will help you to compile the list of materials that you will need and enable you to determine the manufacturing process necessary to produce it. Then you will be able to calculate the manufacturing cost.

- *To arrive at a projected retail price*

When you know the cost of manufacturing you can then determine the cost at retail. Typically the manufacturing cost is about 20 to 25% of the retail price. In other words, if it costs you $5 to manufacture your widget, typically that widget will be sold to retailers like Wal-Mart and Target for about $10. They will retail it for $18.95 to $19.95.

As the manufacturer, you want at least a 50% margin. In order to get a 50% margin you have to mark it up 100% over your cost, which is why what costs you $5 you sell for at least $10.

With those figures in mind, you can now ask related questions:

- *Will the customer pay $20?*
- *What are the competition's products selling for?*

If your product sells for $20 and the competition's sells for $15, not only must you have enough super benefits and features to justify the additional price, but the customer has to perceive that it is worth the extra money. Of course, you think it's worth it. Does the customer?

On the other hand, if your product retails at $20 and the competition's sells at $25, your lower price gives you a competitive advantage and, therefore, a better chance of success.

• *To suggest methods of marketing and distribution*

Understanding the manufacturing and retail costs will help you to plan your market and distribution strategy. A product sold at X price may be better distributed online, for instance, rather than at brick and mortar retail stores. Some retailers will not sell products above or below certain prices because they know their customers and their willingness to pay the price. Some sell to the "high-end market," while others may target the "middle-income" market.

The size or weight of the product also will help you to determine the channels through which it is distributed. For instance, is it so large that you can't put it in a typical retail setting and, therefore, it has to be sold through manufacturing distribution display centers? Or should it be sold strictly online or in some other form or fashion?

Size is an issue because of the retailers' available shelf space and expected return on the space. Weight is an issue as it relates to the ability of the retailers' store personnel, and customers, to move the product around with ease and avoid injury while doing so.

All of these features – price, size, weight – become apparent when you build a prototype.

• *To discover new features to highlight*

In addition to determining the weaknesses and strengths of your invention through testing, you may find that your invention performs functions that you didn't even anticipate or performs those functions far better than you imagined in the concept. You've now just found a new feature to highlight in your marketing campaign.

• *To determine the need for any last-minute design corrections*

If you get your patent and go into production before you build and test a prototype, you may have a real problem if you discover a design flaw that needs to be corrected. I witnessed a good example of this when I owned a logistics company in Indianapolis, a city that is a center for logistics. One of my customers had designed what his company called the "power plate," an exercise device that, when you stand on it, vibrates at high speeds and causes your blood to circulate more rapidly throughout your body, giving you a cardiovascular type of workout in less than two minutes.

112

Chapter 9 - Step 2 of The Simple Plan: Prototype Development

As a logistics provider, my company received his products from China. The first batch we received had a couple of design flaws. One of them, the poorly done paint job, could have been a matter of choosing a bad supplier in China. But the real design flaw came in the operation of the unit due to a problem in the starter. We had to replace the starter in every one of the units in that first batch.

By the time we got the next batch, the starter had been redesigned and was now working fine, but only after my customer spent a lot of money and labor hours correcting his design flaw. Today the product has been totally redesigned and is a beautiful product. It works well and performs a valuable function. But had they built their prototype and tested it thoroughly, they would have discovered the design flaw and corrected it before producing the first batch.

- *To give yourself and others a reason to keep believing in your invention*

Sometimes without a prototype to see, touch, and demonstrate, hope fades. A prototype will help you to keep believing. It can also help you attract investors and partners. It helps you in so many ways when people can see the vision of your product in a tangible form and they can actually use it and gain confirmation that it solves the problem for which it was created, effectively and efficiently.

Who Should Build the Prototype?

Once you've decided to make a prototype of your invention, you have essentially two choices:

- If you're good with your hands, you can find the materials and parts and build it yourself.

- You can have someone else make it for you.

If you intend to make the prototype yourself, ask yourself first whether or not you have the technical savvy, artistic talent, and time to do it correctly. If you have a background in product creation, building, and design, if you can cobble together the right components, you may be able to build it yourself. But be honest with yourself. If you don't know what you're doing, save yourself the time, money, and worry and have someone else do it for you.

If you join or at least inquire with an inventors club or group, they will be able to direct you to local resources that can help you with your prototype.

Part 2 - The Simple Plan

The cost will vary depending on the complexity of your invention.

How I Built My First Prototype

When I was building my prototype for Phase 10, I cobbled together components from other games. You can take components from other products, too. You don't have to build everything from scratch. Your goal is just to make sure your invention works.

I began by buying an Uno card game because I knew that the number of cards in an Uno deck were the same number of cards required in my game and that my game, therefore, would fit in an Uno-sized package.

Uno boxes, back then, were glued along the bottom. At the time, they were red on the outside and white on the inside. I unglued the box, then turned it inside out and re-glued it. Now the box was white.

I then placed the Uno deck back in the package and closed it. I inserted the Uno cards because I hadn't yet begun production so, of course, I didn't have Phase 10 cards. But, because the two games both used the same number of cards, the Uno cards gave the package the same weight so, as I demonstrated it to people, they could get a feel for the actual weight Phase 10 would be in production.

Next, I had an artist friend transfer the design of the Phase 10 game package directly onto this now-white box and then I shrink-wrapped it. Shrink wrap is the clear film in which a game typically is wrapped. My prototype now looked just like a production copy ready to be sold in a store.

When I took it to Kmart, I hadn't yet produced a single unit of the game. I told him: "This is what it's *going* to look like. This is what it's *going* to feel like. Here's the design. Here's the package. Here's the verbiage that's on the package." And do you know what? He bought it! Only then did I go into production, *after* I got my first order.

I got my first order from Meijer at that time also. It was August 10, 1982, when I shipped my first production copies of Phase 10 to both retailers. I had already landed two large retailers before I'd gone into production. And that was done on the strength of a prototype!

My point here is that prototypes can help you land customers, help you land investors, help you determine the form and function of your invention, and help you make certain the concept is sound and that it actually performs the way you expect it to.

Watch Out for Pitfalls and Sign an NDA

If you do contract someone else to make your prototype for you, be aware of these few pitfalls:

- Make sure you pay for their services – and get a receipt. You don't want them coming back later saying that they have shared ownership because you didn't pay for the prototype and you don't have a receipt to prove it.

- Put in writing exactly what you want them to build and all requirements of the prototype. If you have any drawings or sketches, share them. The bottom line here is you want to make sure you're on the same page as your builder.

- Be sure you have a good understanding of what's going to happen and how much it's going to cost.

Finally, require any and all contractors to sign non-disclosure agreements (NDA) so that they are legally bound to keep everything about your invention confidential.

Also, a work-for-hire (WFH) agreement is helpful here. It protects you from contractors who try to claim ownership of your invention and/or any additions or improvements they come up with. Even if you use a work-for-hire agreement, if they add a patentable element, they must be named as a co-inventor in the patent application. However, in the work-for-hire agreement, you can stipulate that they are "assigning" any rights in the patent and patentable elements they created to you or your company. With this agreement, therefore, you will own and control anything they contribute to your invention.

Samples of NDA and WFH agreements can be found through a Google search or on my website at www.thesimpleplan.com

Materials Used to Build Prototypes

There are many types of material that you can use to build your prototype. Following is a sample of common types:

Wood and Clay

Some prototypes, depending on their complexity, are actually carved out of wood. Others are molded out of clay. Today, automotive manufacturers build huge clay models of car designs.

Plastics

When I first started inventing products over forty years ago, if you had a toy that was made of plastic, you generally made your prototype out of plastic. The process was often expensive. In today's environment there are so many relatively inexpensive ways to build prototypes, even using plastic. 3D printed prototypes are made of plastics.

Borrow Other Products/Modify Existing Parts

I showed you how I used an Uno game as the foundation of my prototype. You can do the same. Do you need an electrical switch? A circuit board? A spring? You can find parts that are almost exactly what you need from other products and modify them to fit your needs. If you can find the right size, the right form, the right fit in another product, use it for your prototype.

That's what I did when I turned the Uno box inside out and had the Phase 10 graphics drawn directly on the new outside of the package. However, times have changed from when I started over forty years ago. New methods have been invented.

3D Printing

Rapid prototyping, or what's called 3D printing, is not possible for every invention. But when it is possible, it is probably the best method and the least expensive route to building a firm, functioning prototype. It's fast; you have a finished prototype within hours. It's far less expensive than it was twenty years ago when you had to build molds and plastic injection. Also, by using 3D printing, you can build a prototype to scale, including one that requires a few moving parts.

To view a video that demonstrates how 3D printing actually works, I invite you to check out my website at www.thesimpleplan.com

Chapter 9 - Step 2 of The Simple Plan: Prototype Development

Conclusion

Without conducting a research evaluation of the market (*The Simple Plan*, step 1) and a product evaluation of your prototype, referred to in the next chapter, the other steps to *The Simple Plan* are a waste of time and money. Take your time and review this chapter. Review your prototype options carefully. Get a good feel for its market potential based on your product, considering what its form and function are all about, and determine what prototyping method will work best for your invention.

Chapter 10

Step 3 of The Simple Plan:

Product Evaluation

"Success isn't the result of spontaneous combustion.
You must set yourself on fire."
Arnold Glasow

"The pessimist sees difficulty in every opportunity.
The optimist sees opportunity in every difficulty."
Winston Churchill

Product evaluation is similar to the research evaluation of step one in terms of how you do it. However, its focus is in different areas. In this step you will be evaluating primarily the prototype and its various aspects including the manufacturing of it, its cost, and how well it performs during testing. Also, you will seek out the consumer's response to your prototype's function.

Avoiding Dangerous Territory

After you've built the prototype and it has been tested, you need to evaluate, first, if the market is interested in your product and, second, if the retail price is right. The results of this critical third step in *The Simple Plan*, the product evaluation, will determine whether or not you can proceed with the fourth and fifth steps, PPA and intellectual property registration, and then continue further to licensing or venturing your invention.

The research evaluation, which you read about in step one, and product evaluation, which you'll learn about in this chapter, are the most critical steps in the inventing process. They're more important than the prototype, more important than the patent, more important than the licensing or venturing. Why is that?

Because without a proper evaluation of your invention, you are proceeding blindly into dangerous territory. If the evaluation steps demonstrate that there's no market for your invention, no commercial potential for success, then you will find out before you waste a lot of time and money.

Testing Your Prototype

During the product evaluation, you must have potential users test your prototype. Your goal is to determine how well it performs and what the users think of its effectiveness and efficiency.

Have every volunteer sign a non-disclosure agreement (NDA). You can then have them test the invention prototype in any of several ways. Testing could be done by:

- Formal focus groups: You can find and hire a company that provides this level of testing.
- Friends and family: Make sure that they judge the invention impartially.
- Experts in the industry of your product: Ask buyers, retailers, distributors, manufacturers' reps, engineers, and others.
- General consumers of your product: Any person who would use your product to solve a problem or fill a need.

Questions to Ask

In each case, you want them to examine and use, when possible, the prototype and answer the following questions:

- Did the invention solve your problem or fill your need?
- Did it solve the problem to your satisfaction?
- Was the solution effective?
- Was it efficient?
- Did it function well?
- Did it do the job?
- Did it do it well?
- How did its performance compare to the product that you are currently using to solve the problem?
- Was it easy or difficult to learn to use?

Finally:

- Would you buy it?
- How much would you pay?

Other Questions

You can ask other questions beyond those listed here. This is just a starting point. Be specific to your product and its industry.

When asking them to compare your product against others currently on the market, some of the comparative factors include cost, performance, ease of use, size and compactness, and durability. What factors are likely to be important to your customer base? Ask your testers.

The benefits of your invention should be fairly obvious. You can demo it to a small crowd but demos in a retail setting are hard to arrange and imagine how much harder it is to demo it to an international audience, on a consistent basis. If the benefits are not obvious when the customer looks at it, they should be explainable in one or two sentences. The package can and should proclaim the benefits as well. The more obvious the benefits are, the more likely you will be to have success in the marketplace.

Here are two more important product evaluation questions:

- Is your product clearly new and different?
- How so?

If you can answer yes to the first question, and if your product is perceived by the customer to be cost-effective and beneficial, then you have a potential homerun.

Price alone is seldom a determining factor. But, if two products offer the same features and benefits and one is significantly lower in price, it could be the determinant in that case. A lower price will generally put that product ahead of its competition if all other factors are equal.

Here are three more questions you want your testers to answer for you:

- Does your product have emotional appeal?
- Does it make them happy?
- Do they get excited to use it?

Part 2 - The Simple Plan

When I was inventing my games, my goal was for them to make the people who played them happy. Happiness was the emotion that I was trying to bring out. Game manufacturers want to get customers emotionally involved when playing their games. What emotion do you want your users to feel?

Aggravation, for instance, doesn't sound like a good emotion, but, from a game manufacturer's perspective, it causes people to want to do better next time. Sometimes that hooks people. It causes them to be addicted, always striving to do better.

So, an emotion that may not seem positive in normal day-to-day life can actually have a positive impact on a game. That emotion could be happiness. It could be satisfaction. It could be joy. It could be relief. It could be any other emotion that causes consumers to be attracted to your product and want to use it continually.

Even if the emotion on the surface appears to be negative, if it keeps your customers coming back again and again, that's a good thing from a marketing perspective. I sought also to have my game players interact with one another on some level. Games are designed to be social. Interaction brings about communication.

Does your product have an acceptable price/value relationship?

You want your product to be priced well. Your customers must see the price and the value as being equal. Better yet if they see the value as being greater than the price.

One question you could ask to determine the price/value relationship is: If you could buy this product at $_____ price (a price appropriate for your invention), would that price be worthwhile to you?

If they say, "Yeah, I would pay $200; I would pay $300," that tells you they see it at a greater value than even the price dictates. If they can see the value and the price as being on at least equal levels, you have a shot in the marketplace. You have an even greater chance of success if value is perceived to be on a higher level than price. In that case, your customers will see themselves as getting a great value at a low price.

Key Factors to Evaluate Your Invention/Product

Many factors will affect the marketability of your invention. Each may affect it to a different degree. Some factors may affect it barely at all for this invention but greatly for a later invention.

There are no guarantees that your invention will be a success. But if you do the product evaluation properly and objectively, which includes paying attention to these key factors, you increase its likelihood of success.

Let's look at those key factors now.

Cost

The cost of your invention both during manufacturing and at retail can determine your invention's likelihood of success. When you build a prototype, you learn what materials are involved and what's required to manufacture your invention. Once you have the material cost information, you can calculate its cost to manufacture. Typically, your retail cost is between four and five times the manufacturing cost. The difference between the manufacturing cost and the wholesale price to retailers is called the "markup."

Once you know the retail price, you can ask your testers if they will pay it. If your manufacturing cost is so high that it renders a retail cost out of reach for the consumer, then you have a problem. You have to look at the cost, both in manufacturing and at retail.

Weight

What is the weight of the invention? This may not sound like a big deal, but the weight will help to determine the shipping cost, which is a component of the eventual retail price. In addition, weight could be an issue in terms of its consumer usability. Heavier products are more difficult to handle. Lightweight products are usually preferred by consumers.

Retailers also may have an issue with the weight of the invention/product. The weight may affect how it is displayed in their store and if it can be displayed.

Size

What is the size of your invention relative to competing products in the marketplace? Size "will matter" at retail as well. Is the invention too large for shelf space? Or is it too large for retail display in its product category? If it can't be displayed along with competing products at retail, because of its size, you have a problem.

Health and Safety

Does your invention cause health concerns for your consumer? How about safety issues? Does it raise concerns about liability? Prospective licensees will want to know.

Speed

Speed of production: Can your product be produced in an efficient manner?

Speed in use: Is it fast to use? Or, does it require more time in its uses?

Ease of Use

Can a person easily use your invention? Does it require educating the user? If so, you could have a problem, especially if your competition's product is easier to use and learn how to use.

Easily Perceived Benefits

Can users of your invention perceive its benefit just by looking at it or using it? If so, your likelihood of success will increase. The ease of use and the visible factors or benefits are important.

Ease of Production

When your invention goes into production or manufacture, you want it to be easy to produce. The more difficult it is to produce, the more it's going to cost to manufacture. That means it will cost more at retail and could get priced out of reach of the consumer's budget.

Bear in mind that consumers have a price range they're willing to pay for any solution, no matter how well it works and whether or not there is competition in the marketplace.

Availability of Production Materials

In addition to your invention being easy to produce, the materials needed to produce it need to be readily available and not too expensive. Low availability means high price. High availability means low price.

Durability

Will your invention last? For some products, durability isn't a big issue.

But it usually is in most cases.

You can look at my card game, for instance, Phase 10. It's as durable as other card games. But even durable card games wear out; and the more you play them, the sooner they become unusable. Everybody understands that about cards. They know the cards will eventually wear out.

That outcome is acceptable when it comes to cards, but it may not be acceptable in your industry. Your product most likely will need to be more durable than cards in a card deck. You can determine lifespan expectations and what's acceptable by looking at similar products in your industry, especially those products of your direct competition.

Repairability

Not every product is repairable; when it breaks down, you have to replace it. If your product has a repairable factor associated with it, you need to make certain it is easily repairable. Consumers will feel good about buying your product when they know that repairs can be done as needed, either professionally or Do It Yourself.

Reliability

Will your product be reliable and trustworthy? Will it perform effectively and efficiently? Reliability is important with most inventions, particularly those that have a utility involvement. People want to make sure that it works and does what it's supposed to do. The reliability of your product will be determined while you are testing your prototype and then in further testing of your production units.

Sell-ability

How difficult is it to sell your product? We talked earlier about the benefits of your product. If the benefits are apparent and readily perceivable, then sell-ability is easy. If the benefits are not so apparent, then sell-ability becomes more difficult.

Without sell-ability, you have to invest time and resources to demonstrate and prove the benefits, to convince people that they need it. Therefore, you want the benefits of your invention/product to be apparent to reduce or eliminate costs to educate the consumer and increase its sell-ability.

Appearance

While appearance obviously is important, the aesthetics of certain products are more important than the aesthetics of others. Look at the appearance of competing products, and of other products in your industry. In what ways, if any, is appearance important? How is it less so? How important is appearance overall? You want to design an appearance for your product that looks good and is pleasing and attractive to your users.

Precision

Precision is important while your product is being manufactured and again when it is being used. Is your invention easy to use? Does it do the job effectively and efficiently? These are questions that relate to precision. This is true for all inventions but particularly for technical inventions and those with a lot of moving parts, those heavy on the technical and utility side of the invention spectrum.

Noise

Does your invention make more noise in its operation than its competitors? Can you find a way to reduce the noise without raising the price? Being noisier is seldom a benefit and almost always a detriment. If your product is quieter or runs more smoothly than its competition, you are at a decided advantage. If it's noisier than the competition, you are at a disadvantage.

Odor

If your invention has an unpleasing odor to it, you have a problem. I was watching *Shark Tank* one night. A gentleman had come up with an invention that had an awful odor. All the sharks noticed the odor, which was not meant to be an element of the product. I mean, it wasn't a benefit or a feature of the product. It was a terrible byproduct or consequence, you might say.

If your invention has an unpleasing odor, it will face stiff competition from its better-smelling competitors. On the other hand, if it has a pleasing odor and aesthetics, its likelihood of success increases.

Market Size

Do you have a small local market that depends on walk-in traffic? Or do you market your products and services online to an international audience?

Chapter 10 - Step 3 of The Simple Plan: Product Evaluation

Having a big market means your product will appeal to a broader audience. It will be easier for you to find your target consumer. The larger the number of potential users, the greater your chance of success.

A small market means there will be a ceiling on profits. If there already is a lot of competition, breaking into the market may be more difficult. You'll have to carefully identify those people receptive to your product, target them, and reach them. It can be done. Sometimes, like when you've invented a specialized product for a specific market, finding and connecting to your market niche is your primary ongoing strategy.

Demand Trend

The trend is the direction that the demand for your particular product is moving. Identify your trend. Is it going up or is it declining? Is it stagnant? Also, be objective. Understand what you're doing. Be honest with yourself. Don't be afraid. You need this knowledge. Without it, you could be wasting your time and your money. Remember, our goal, in doing the evaluation, is to save you from wasting time and money pursuing an invention that has no real market potential.

Once you understand the demand, whatever the result of your research shows doesn't have to be a detriment. Even if the market is declining, understand what's happening and why. With that understanding, you can best determine whether and how to proceed.

Seasonal Demand

A lot of products are seasonal. Winter coats and shovels, for instance, are used throughout the winter but seldom in the summer. Lawn mowers are used more in the summer. Pipes get clogged year round. Understanding your product's seasonal demand helps you to define your customer and plan your marketing strategy.

Difficulty of Market Penetration

Whether you have a big market or a small market, how difficult is it going to be to penetrate it? How strong is your competition? How entrenched are they? How identifiable is their brand? The size and strength of your competition will be a barrier to entry into the marketplace with your new invention but the barrier doesn't have to be impenetrable, as long as you understand what you're up against.

Part 2 - The Simple Plan

Potential Competition

Look objectively at your competition as well as your potential competition, people who are not even in the market yet but may come into it. Determine where the competition is, how they do what they do, and how they are marketing their products.

Studying your competition can give you insight into how to best approach the marketing of your invention. If you decide to license it, everything you learn during your research will help your licensee in approaching the market. If you decide to venture, this insight will help you to approach the market as a business producing your invention/product.

Quality

Obviously, an important factor when it comes to any product is quality. To gain an advantage in the marketplace, the quality of your invention/ product should meet or exceed that of the competition.

Excitement

The more excitement your product generates, the more the likelihood that you'll be successful with it. So be honest in evaluating excitement when you're talking to focus groups and possible users.

- How excited are they when they look at your invention?
- Are they excited when they use it?
- Do they think it helps them solve a problem?

When I was testing Phase 10, I observed people as they played it. I could see they were excited. They were interacting. There was a lot of talk and banter and laughing between them. I knew that I had something. I didn't have to ask them.

However, when testing other games in the same way, I could see the testers were not excited or interacting. I knew from their reaction that I had more work to do.

When people test your prototype, do they get excited over its ability to resolve the problem it was designed to resolve? Where can you make improvements?

Inferior Performance

Now you really have to be honest with yourself. I keep stressing honesty and objectivity because if you find, in testing your prototype, that it is inferior to its competition, or it just does not effectively or efficiently resolve the problem it was designed to resolve, then you need to move on to something else. Don't waste your time or your money dealing with an inferior product – unless you find ways to improve it and can test the improvements.

Either way, you must be honest with yourself and know when to go back to the drawing board.

Sexy Packaging

Sexy packaging is more important to some products than to others. You want your package design to look good, cause people to become excited to buy, grab their attention and show or demonstrate the benefits of its use.

Long Life Cycle

I talked earlier about a product's durability. How durable it is affects its life cycle, which is the amount of time a consumer can assume that it will work. Whether or not you offer your customers a warranty, and the kind of warranty you offer if you do, will be based on what statistics and anecdotes show the durability of your product to be.

For example, in my industry, the life cycle of card games depends greatly on how often they are used. As you know, playing cards do wear out. The consumer understands this. Life cycle is not assumed to be long for card games.

But if my cards wore out after playing only two games, I'd have a problem. This is because most cards are more durable than that and, therefore, have longer life cycles. What's the acceptable life cycle of your product?

Related or Derivative Products

If customers like your product, its success will increase your brand awareness in a positive way. Customers will become more likely to look at related products from you, known as derivative products or brand extensions.

For inventors like you, these offspring of the original mean more income and recognition. As I have mentioned, I've created eight versions of Phase 10, all based on the original but each addressed to a different audience. What derivatives can you create from your product?

Legality

Obviously, your invention must be legal to make, use, transport, and sell. Don't underestimate the importance of this detail.

Operability

Can the average consumer operate your product? Keep this in mind while you're designing it. I mean, obviously, you've invented something for people to buy and use. If they can't use it, they won't buy it.

Keep in mind, as you are developing your product, the consumer who eventually will be using it. Is he or she an average consumer who can use your product with no or limited instruction? Or is your product one that only trained specialists will be able to operate?

Different products require different levels of training to become operable. The key for your product is that it must be operable by its intended user. Instructions must be complete and easy to follow. Diagrams must be accurate and clear.

Development Potential

Can it be developed to its full potential and are you the person to do it? Inventors are great at coming up with the concept for the invention and then many do not feel they can develop it beyond that stage. You must determine whether you can move your invention beyond the idea or concept stage. If not, seek the help of others you trust and who possess the skills you may lack.

Profitability

Can it be made and then sold at a profit? This question goes back to the cost factors we talked about earlier. Profitability is a critical factor in the development of your invention.

Any licensee who has already made a huge investment in the tooling and preparation for manufacture of your product and has not yet recouped any of the investment will not be happy to learn, too late, about superior products that are already on the drawing board or can be foreseen.

Obsolescence

Will your product become obsolete quickly? That's not good if your licensee has made a huge investment in the tooling and preparation for manufacture of it. If it becomes obsolete before he's recouped his initial investment because superior products are already on the drawing board or can be foreseen, that's a problem.

Fad items don't face the problem of obsolescence. Those products are only expected to last a few months or years, maybe even only a couple of seasons. Everyone understands that and your licensee will plan for its eventual decline.

Instant Obsolescence

Some products take so long to get to market, from concept to market, that by the time they reach the market they are already obsolete. Perhaps the technology is moving so fast they can't keep up with it. Or else its consumers are so fickle that they move around from product to product too quickly to develop loyalty to any particular product. Is your product a candidate for instant obsolescence?

Product Liability Risk

The more likely your product is to pose a health or safety hazard, and the more serious the hazard is likely to be, the higher will be your product's liability risk.

When your product goes to market, you're going to need liability insurance. If your product has a high liability risk, you will find yourself carrying high insurance premiums. If your product becomes a huge safety hazard, you could find yourself out of business because you can't obtain liability insurance or won't be able to afford to fight the lawsuits resulting from a high-risk product. Also note that licensees tend to shy away from products that are a huge risk of liability.

Difficulty of Distribution

How difficult is it to get your products into the distribution channels that will carry them from the factory into users' hands.

The answer is based on a few factors. How entrenched is the competition in your industry? How much shelf space is available in each method or channel of distribution?

It's hard to get product placement space in grocery stores, for instance. In other industries, such as specialty retailers, it's not as difficult to find a retailer willing to take your product, assuming it's good, obviously.

What will be your method or channel of distribution?

Service Requirement

Will your invention require a lot of service or any service at all? If it will, you will want to prepare a contingency plan. You may have to develop a network of service dealers or make do-it-yourself equipment or parts available for customers to service the product themselves. What service requirements are necessary? Will it be necessary to provide repair or service documentation?

Production Facilities

Can your invention be produced? Are there facilities readily available that have the equipment, the resources, and the capacity to produce your invention?

Radically Different

Ideally, your product's benefits and how to use your product are readily perceivable.

If your product is so radically different from people's experience that they can't even imagine how to use it or perceive its benefits, then it may require a demonstration or an explanation. If this is the case, you may have to distribute the product via infomercial, shopping channels, online using demo videos, or through a retailer that is able and willing to provide the personnel to demo the product.

Minor or Great Technical Advancement

If your invention represents a great technical advance, it may be difficult to produce. This is because the production equipment may not exist or the cost of production makes it too costly for retail. Users may have a hard time perceiving or learning how to use it. You may face challenges getting it into distribution. Minor advances may not matter to the customers.

Difficult/Easy to Promote

If your invention is difficult to promote, obviously that's an issue. If it's easy to promote, then that's obviously an advantage.

Presence of Market

One of the main reasons for going through the product evaluation process is to determine the likelihood of marketability or commercial success. If you find only a slight market for the invention, you may want to move on to one of your other ideas. The broader your product's market appeal is, the more likely it will be successful. How broad is your market?

Crowded Market or Wide Open Field

How crowded is the market for your invention? What level of competition do you face?

If there's a crowded market, you've got an issue. If there is not a whole lot of competition or if the competition is spread out so that no one has a strong market share, then you're in an open market and you could take advantage of it.

* * *

That's it! All of the above factors should be reviewed and tested as they relate to your invention. Which areas are weak but can be strengthened? Which are serious enough to cause you to kill your invention outright? Be honest and objective so that you can make the best decision in pursuing your invention to success, or putting it back on the shelf and moving on to your next invention.

Another purpose for the list is to give you a way to compare two of your inventions for relative value, so that you know where to concentrate effort and resources at this time.

Name Value

Does your product have a great name or other promotional possibilities?

You want to come up with a name for your product that is catchy and can be trademarked. I'll discuss trademarks in more detail in chapter 12 on intellectual property.

For now, keep in mind that a great product name lends itself to great promotional and branding possibilities that will differentiate your product from its competition.

Examples of product names I've used for my games include Phase 10, Stake Your Stash, and Caught Cha. I looked for names that were different from other games out there. I researched to make certain that I could trademark the names because I wanted to build a brand around them.

When I came up with Phase 10, I was in my apartment. I remember it well. I was sitting on the edge of my bed and thinking, "Okay, what am I going to call this game?" My first thought, knowing that the winner is the first player to accomplish ten steps, was "10 Steps." It was simple, obvious, and straightforward. But—remember, you have to be honest and objective—it wasn't very catchy. I mean, it just didn't do anything for me.

Then I thought, why don't I just switch the order and call it "Step 10"? I liked that better! It was different, a little catchy, and I didn't think I would have any trouble getting a trademark registration for it. But I still wasn't satisfied. I thought some more and I started seeing synonyms: "10 steps, 10 aspects, 10 things you must complete, 10 phases you must go through. Ten phases! Phase 10!" The name just presented itself after a relaxed round of free association and creative word play.

From there, it took off. I was able to get a trademark registration. Now it's a brand name in the Toy and Game world and it stands out on its own.

Start thinking of names while you're going through the product evaluation, so that you can share them with your testers. Come up with five potential names. Then ask your testers to rate them on a scale of 1 (hate it) to 10 (love it) or rank them in order of favorability. Ask open-ended questions about each name so your testers can deepen their evaluations: What do you like best and least about it?

Research Panel or Board

If you can find individuals who have some background in the industry, are good at marketing, or have some expertise in product development, you might consider inviting them to be on your "research panel." They can be your impartial board of advisors to help you as you develop your invention and bring it to market.

Of course, anyone who reviews your product should first sign a non-disclosure agreement.

Examples of industry insiders include:

- Retail buyers
- Manufacturers' representatives
- Industry distributors
- Marketing experts in the industry
- Store owners

Ask them if they would be willing to sit down with you and help you as you develop and test your invention and research the market. Most people will offer you help and answer a few questions at no cost. So, first, see if they will just answer a few questions.

But if you want to have them involved on a regular basis to give you in-depth, detailed input whenever you want it, you may need to pay them a little something. I've never paid for this kind of help. However, I've seen other inventors do it to good ends.

In either case, it is certainly helpful to have an industry insider who is available to mentor you.

Retail buyers can help by offering you insight into the needs of retailers, what is going on in the retail world, and what competitors are doing to fill the needs of the market. They will also know best what your packaging should look like to appeal to both retail buyers and the public.

Manufacturers' reps will have insight into the overall sentiment of retail buyers and manufacturers.

Industry distributors will, like manufacturers' reps, know both retail buyer and manufacturer sentiments and can provide a broad range of guidance related to both.

Marketing experts in your industry will be able to tell you what the overall market is related to the consumers of your product.

Store owners can give you insight into what's going on in the retail world,

Part 2 - The Simple Plan

what store owners and buyers are seeing out there, what products are coming, and which ones are achieving success.

Trade Shows

Most industries have annual trade shows. If yours does, I definitely recommend that you attend them. Some industries have multiple trade shows annually. Try to attend the biggest or the one closest to you.

At trade shows you can compile information on the industry, meet insiders, learn about trends, and see what your competition is doing. You can seek mentors and others who can answer industry insider questions for you.

I was well on the way to launching my early products before I was aware that there were trade shows. I found out about the New York Toy Fair from Mr. Christensen just before I got Dice Baseball on the market. I didn't attend Toy Fair until after Phase 10 was on the market and being sold by Kmart and Meijer. The New York Toy Fair was then and still may be the biggest trade show available in the toy industry. It's held every February in New York City.

However, upon attending I found many potential suppliers at Toy Fair. I was able to see what other products were coming soon. I met and began to develop relationships with insiders who were able to help me and give me guidance. I was now a part of the toy and game community! In looking back, I would have gone to Toy Fair from day one if I had known about it, I learned so much from the experience.

Find the industry association related to your product. It can give you information about trade shows and other insider information about the industry. You just want to ask general questions when you're talking to people on this level. You aren't yet revealing the details of your invention.

Conclusion

The product evaluation is very important to your invention's success. Take the time to perform this step and be very honest with yourself.

Remember, review the key factors listed in this chapter and determine which apply to your invention. Then honestly assess how your invention stacks up to each that apply.

Finally, make certain to have potential consumers of your invention assess it and provide you with insights into its commercial potential.

Chapter 11

Step 4 of The Simple Plan:

Provisional Patent Application (PPA)

"Success consists of going from failure to failure without loss of enthusiasm." Winston Churchill

"A great pleasure in life is doing what people say you cannot do." Walter Bagehot

Let me give you my disclaimer before I begin this chapter. I am not a patent attorney or an attorney of any kind. The information that I give you here about provisional patent applications, or PPAs, and intellectual property rights is based on my research, experience, and observations as a professional inventor for forty years, but it isn't legal advice. Before you act on anything you learn here related to PPA's and intellectual property rights, consult with your patent attorney. Okay? That's my disclaimer.

* * *

If you've already determined that you will want to file a patent ultimately on your invention; and you've completed the first three steps, built a prototype, and tested it, first by yourself, then with a few close friends and relatives, and then with a broader group of potential users of the invention; and you've gotten all of them to sign non-disclosure agreements and promise to keep everything about your invention confidential, then now is the time to file your provisional patent application (PPA).

If you plan to require your licensee to file a patent application, you also may want to file a PPA at this time.

This is the time, after the product evaluation, when those inventors wanting a patent should file a PPA. That is why it appears in this book following the product evaluation.

However, there are exceptions. Sometimes, you will file the PPA before you do the product evaluation.

For instance, you may *already know that you will want to file a regular utility patent application* and you want a very large test audience of your prototype. If that's the case, you may want to get "protection" by filing a PPA before you have focus groups, potential users, people in the supply chain, potential retailers, and others who may be able to provide meaningful feedback by evaluating it.

In that case, you will flip the order and file a PPA before you do the product evaluation. For most other inventors, the PPA comes after the product evaluation.

What Is a PPA?

A provisional patent application is not in itself a patent. It does not give you any patent rights. It's simply an application filed ahead of the regular utility application. Like a placeholder, it sets your priority date for a regular utility application to follow any time within one year of the date you file the PPA.

For example, if you file a PPA on August 15 of one year, then that will be the date of your regular utility application that you must file any time within a year of that August 15 date. If you file your regular utility application on July 1 the following year and a patent is issued, your utility patent will be deemed to have the August 15 filing date.

Summary: Once you file for a PPA, you have one year to determine the potential success of your invention while reserving your priority date for a utility application to follow later.

Why File a PPA?

There are two reasons why you may want to file the PPA before proceeding with the product evaluation.

1) You ultimately want to apply for a *regular utility patent* but you aren't ready yet. Filing a regular utility patent application can be very expensive. The PPA will give you time to explore the potential of your invention before bearing the expense of a regular patent application.

138

2) During the product evaluation phase, you will be talking about and showing the prototype to potential users, people involved in the supply chain, retailers, distributors, and others, and you want to be able to tell them the "patent is pending." In this way, you demonstrate a level of "perceived ownership." For those of you who are "paranoid inventors," you won't have to worry about anyone stealing your idea at this point because you will have already filed a provisional patent application, which gives you "patent pending" status.

Nevertheless, you'll want them to sign an NDA, because you still want to keep your invention confidential and you don't want to make it public.

If you are not yet concerned about a patent, then you'll do the product evaluation first and decide later whether or not to file the PPA, in part based on the results of your product evaluation.

What Is in a PPA?

A PPA must contain a detailed description of the invention, including how to build it and use it. How detailed must it be? It must disclose all of the elements of your invention.

If necessary, it will also contain drawings designed to facilitate understanding of the description. You can do the work yourself or hire a patent attorney. Along with the description, you will submit a cover letter or cover sheet that includes some basic information about the inventors, the invention, and other required information. All of the requirements of a PPA filing are listed on the USPTO.gov website.

You will pay either a micro entity fee or a small entity fee. The fee range is between $65 and $130. As an independent inventor, you're probably qualified for the micro entity fee of $65. If you file a PPA yourself, this will be your only fee.

However, if you hire a patent attorney to do all the work, make the drawings, write the description, and write the claims, you will incur more expense.

Many inventors file the PPA themselves. It's not difficult and can save you a lot of money. There are several books available that will walk you through the entire process. I'd recommend you check one out if filing a PPA yourself is something you want to do. Also, there is software provided by a law firm that you can use to prepare a PPA yourself. Check it out at www.patentwizard.com/

Go to my website for the latest info regarding DIY filing of a PPA: www.thesimpleplan.com

What a PPA Is NOT

A PPA is not a regular patent. It's not even a regular patent application (RPA). Some people refer to it as a "provisional patent" but this is incorrect. It's simply a placeholder for the regular patent application that will follow within the next year.

A PPA *cannot* by itself result in a patent. It does not require a patent application declaration or an information disclosure statement. Patent claims are not required, although many PPA's include them. An abstract and summary are not required, nor is a description of the invention's background or a statement of its objectives and advantages.

But if you don't file an RPA within a year of your PPA's filing date, your PPA will be considered abandoned and will become forever useless.

I said in the section above that the PPA must disclose all of the elements of your invention. What it cannot include are any additional elements you develop after its filing. So it's important to be accurate and complete when you file your PPA.

And that's why I think it's important to file the PPA after you've built your prototype, tested it, and proven the concept. During those stages you will often discover elements of your invention that need to be altered, changed, corrected, or modified.

Now, as I've said, there are exceptions where you will file the PPA before building the prototype. The most common exceptions are when your prototype will be very expensive to build or if your invention is very complicated.

However, if it's going to take you more than a year to build and test the prototype, then filing a PPA is a waste of money.

What a PPA Accomplishes

A PPA establishes your invention's priority in an interference proceeding. An interference is a procedure conducted by the United States Patent and

Trademark Office (USPTO) to decide which of two or more pending patent applications claiming the same product or invention should receive the patent. If your priority date is earlier, generally you will receive the patent, according to United States law.

When you ultimately file your RPA, sometime within twelve months of filing the PPA, your priority date, the date of filing, will be shown to be your date of filing for the PPA – if, of course, you've fully disclosed and provided the same claims and concepts in both the PPA and RPA.

A PPA antedates any publication of the invention because if you publish your invention, make it known, before filing, it could be considered "prior art," which would make it impossible for you to get a patent. Thus it is important to keep your invention confidential and not made public in any way.

"Prior art" is any evidence that your invention is already known. Prior art does not need to exist physically or be commercially available. It is enough that you or someone, somewhere, sometime previously has described or shown or made something that contains a use of technology or utility that you claim to have invented known to the public in any way.

Patent Pending Status

The PPA also gives you the right to claim that your invention has patent pending status. On any documentation and on the invention itself, you can write "Patent Pending."

Patent pending status helps you in your marketing to potential licensees and in your negotiations with them if you get to that stage. They will understand that you have not yet filed an RPA. The PPA also helps you to ward off potential infringers because they will see patent pending status on your invention and related documents, and recognize that a patent may be coming.

You get these advantages without the expense of an RPA. In common parlance, this means that you can confidently publish, sell, or show your invention to others without fear of theft or loss of any domestic rights. Anyone who "steals" your invention now will have a later filing date than yours so you would almost certainly win any interference with that thief.

Part 2 - The Simple Plan

Disadvantages of a PPA

If your PPA fails to contain a full description of the actual "nuts and bolts" of your invention and you correct the description in your RPA, you will lose the PPA filing date as your priority date for any purpose related to your invention. That's why it's so important that your PPA be complete and accurate. And that's why, for most people, who have not gone through any training and do not understand the process thoroughly, it's probably a good idea to hire a patent attorney to do it, at a cost of probably between $1,000 and $2,000.

Or you can hire a registered patent agent to file it for you at a cost that will not be super expensive. There are two types of registered practitioners before the patent office: patent agents and patent attorneys.

> • Patent agents have only their registered practitioner credential, which means that they are only allowed to practice patent law before the patent office.

> • Patent attorneys can practice patent law and engage in other forms of legal representation, such as preparing and negotiating licensing agreements, and representing parties in court. In addition to having the registered practitioner credential from the patent office, a patent attorney will have a law degree and be a member in good standing of a bar association.

In the eyes of the patent office, a patent attorney and a patent agent are the same. Both can represent you throughout your patent application process. Only in the areas outside the patent office is there a difference.

Although patent agents are limited to just practicing before the patent office, they can still be excellent at what they do. Also, many patent agents have experience on the technical side of invention and not just the patent writing side. Since they are limited to practicing before the patent office, they are usually less expensive than a full-blown patent attorney.

Other Disadvantages of a PPA

Two other disadvantages of a PPA:

> • You may unintentionally forego foreign protection because you

142

cannot wait one year after filing the RPA as is usually done to foreign file. Instead, you must make both your foreign filing decision and your regular U.S. filing decision within one year after your PPA is filed. Consult your attorney for more details if you want to file foreign patents. There are timing issues you must be aware of before disclosing your invention publicly.

- You must try to license or interest a manufacturer in your invention in the approximately ten-month period between when you file the PPA and when you must begin preparing the RPA so that you can complete the RPA in the final two months of the twelve-month deadline. Since ten months may not be enough time to find and engage a licensee, you may get discouraged, fail to file the RPA, and lose your priority date afforded by the PPA.

Should You File a PPA?

If you ultimately want to file a regular utility patent, then I recommend that you file a PPA, especially if you are not in a position to build and test your prototype, perhaps due to its high cost.

If you wish to establish an early filing date, since you feel your invention is potentially valuable and might be independently developed by others or stolen from you, you may want to go ahead and file the PPA. If you're concerned about theft, if you're concerned about someone else independently coming up with the same idea, go ahead and get your PPA filed.

Public Disclosure

A public disclosure of your invention has occurred when:

- You put it on the Internet
- It's been written up in an article
- You've built a prototype and started trying to sell the product "anywhere": on the Internet, at flea markets, to retailers, and any other sales outlets.

Anything you've done publicly will be viewed by the patent office as "prior art" and starts the clock ticking. You have one year to file your RPA or you will lose your right to file for a patent forever.

Part 2 - The Simple Plan

How to Prepare and File a PPA

Your PPA must be well written. That's why an attorney would be helpful. Attorneys know all the legalese and what should be written and how it should be written. Use any legal terms that are acceptable or required. It should be typed in a specific format.

To prepare and file a PPA, you must complete these steps:

- Prepare drawings.
- Prepare a complete description of the structure and operation of the invention.
- Prepare a cover letter and fee transmittal.
- Prepare any needed small entity declarations.
- Attach a check for the filing fee and the necessary postcard.
- Mail all papers to the PTO.

Details of all the above are provided by the patent office on its website: USPTO.gov.

The particular aspects of the PPA are very, very important.

Conclusion

A PPA may not apply specifically to your needs or concerns. You may not be interested in filing a regular patent application, so none of this information will be necessary for you.

However, the goal here is to give you an overview of how a PPA works, what it looks like, why it's used, and when it's used. If you have an invention that you ultimately want to get a patent on, then file the PPA and buy yourself some time. If you are not concerned about a patent or a patent does not apply to your invention, then the PPA is not necessary.

If you are one of the exceptions, you may file the PPA before building and testing a prototype. But for 95% of the inventors out there, build a prototype before filing a PPA. Get people who review it to sign an NDA, thereby keeping it confidential and preventing it from being made public. Next, test it, make sure it works, ensure that it functions effectively and efficiently. Then file your PPA.

For your specific needs, consult your attorney. Many of them will give you a free consultation during which you can ask them questions pertinent to your invention.

Chapter 12

Step 5 of The Simple Plan:

Intellectual Property Registration

"Inaction breads doubt and fear. Action breads confidence and courage. If you want to conquer fear, do not sit home and think about it. Go out and get busy." Dale Carnegie

"You must have long-range goals to keep you from being frustrated by short-range failures." Charles Noble

Some of you who are reading this book will not need to register any intellectual property (IP). You may not be interested in a patent. A copyright may not apply to your invention, nor will a trademark. If your invention is an industrial product or part, for instance, you may not need a trademark, and certainly you won't need a copyright. But you may desire to obtain a patent. It will depend on your goals.

In this chapter, I will give you an overview of these three forms of registration so that you can get a feel for what applies to your particular invention. In following chapters, I will look at each form one at a time.

People often think of a patent as protection, but an IP does not "protect" your invention. An IP gives you *offensive rights,* which allow you to prohibit others from producing that particular product or invention, through litigation if necessary. That's all it does. In order to enforce your rights, you usually have to file a lawsuit. That means you have to *spend money* and a lot of time dealing with a lot of attorneys. Even then, the outcome of any litigation is not certain.

Patents

So, exactly what is a patent is and what does it do? There are three specific kinds of patents:

Utility Patent

Part 2 - The Simple Plan

The utility patent is the primary form of patent to which most people are referring when they say they have a patent or are applying for one. A utility patent is the most-applied-for type of patent. It covers inventions that function in a unique manner to produce a utilitarian result. In other words, a utility patent covers the functionality of the invention, how it does what it does, and the components that make up or produce that functionality. This kind of patent lasts seventeen years from the date of issuance or twenty years from the filing date.

Plant Patent

The second form of patent is called a plant patent. Yes, you can patent a plant! A plant patent covers asexually reproducible plants, that is, those plants produced through the use of grafts and cuttings, such as flowers. So, if you figured out a way to graft an apple tree with an orange tree and produce a new kind of fruit, then you can apply for a patent on that fruit and/or process. A plant patent lasts twenty years from the filing date.

Design Patent

A design patent, as opposed to a utility patent, covers the unique ornamental display or visible shape or design of a non-natural object, even if only on a computer screen. The design of your new Nike shoe, for instance, may have a design patent on its design. The design for the new handbag that you just bought for yourself or your spouse was probably patented.

A design patent is far less expensive than the utility patent, and it may be all you need depending on what your product is. For instance, in reference to the design of an athletic shoe, a design patent is what you would get unless it has some unique utility involved in it functionality. Then you might try for both a design and a utility patent.

Copyrights

The government gives an author of any original work of expression the right to exclude others from copying or commercially using that work of expression without proper authorization. This form of IP registration is known as copyright.

Like a patent, a copyright is an offensive right. Even if you haven't published your work, if you've written it and registered the copyright, you can prohibit others from commercially using your work and take them to court if they copy it anyway without your consent.

Chapter 12 - Step 5 of The Simple Plan: Intellectual Property Registration

The key is to register it. In general, registration is voluntary. Copyright exists from the moment the work is created. You will have to register, however, if your copyright is infringed and you wish to bring a lawsuit. You cannot bring a lawsuit for an unregistered copyright. So it is advisable to register.

The U.S. Copyright Office prefers online registration. Cost is $35 for "one work by a single author who is also the claimant and the work is not made for hire." Cost otherwise is $55.

To register and to find answers to your questions, go to www.copyright.gov

Examples of works that are covered by copyright include books, poetry, plays, songs, catalogs, photographs, computer programs, advertisements, labels, movies, maps, drawings, sculpture, prints, art reproductions, game boards, rules, and recordings.

For my games, whether they were card games, board games, or computer games, I obtained copyrights, not patents. Again, a patent covers the functionality of an invention. A game board has no function; you just open the board and it rests on the table or floor.

A beautiful feature of a copyright is that it last the lifetime of the author, plus 70 years, much longer than a traditional patent. Since my games have registered copyrights, my son and his heirs will be able to enjoy the offensive rights that copyright registration provides, even after I'm gone.

Trademarks

Trademark is the most familiar branch of intellectual property law. You see trademarks all the time, on a daily basis. Everyone sees them, uses them, and makes decisions based on expectations of them. They are attached to brand names. You buy a soft drink with the Coca-Cola trademark on the can or bottle because you have an expectation of what that soft drink is going to taste like. Its taste will be consistent with the taste of every other Coca-Cola you have ever bought or ever will buy.

When you buy an Orange Crush soft drink, you know it's going to taste different from Coke because it has a different trademark. If the Orange Crush drink is put in a Coke bottle and you taste what you think is going to be Coke but you discover it's Orange Crush, you will realize the importance of expectation as it relates to a trademark.

Part 2 - The Simple Plan

A trademark on a product assures consumers that their expectations of the product will be met. Whatever they buy under the trademark will be in compliance with their expectations, and their experience with the product. When you go to McDonald's and buy a Big Mac, you expect it to taste like a Big Mac, not a Whopper or a Wendy's Double. When you buy a Cadillac, you expect it to perform and function differently than a Honda Civic.

You probably decided to purchase your newest appliance, much of the food in your kitchen, and your magazines based at least to some extent on trademarks. When you buy a Dell computer, you expect a certain level of quality and functionality from the computer because it has a Dell trademark on it.

You should choose a trademark for your consumer product that will distinguish it from other brands in the marketplace.

In its most literal meaning, a trademark is any word or symbol that is consistently attached to, or forms a part of, a product to identify and distinguish it from others in the marketplace. In other words, it is a brand.

I explained earlier how I chose the name for Phase 10 while I was seeking a trademark that would distinguish it from other card games.

So again, we make decisions on a daily basis based on our expectations of the trademarks and brands with which we've become familiar because of their respective levels of consistency.

Brand Consistency

Within any brand, you expect consistency.

Years ago, one of my licensees decided to create an electronic handheld version of Phase 10. It was launched before I had the chance to review and approve it. Well, they made one change in the instructions that caused the game to play slightly differently from the original card game.

Because it was marketed as an "electronic version" of the original card game, consumers expected it to have the same gameplay as the original card game. Due to the change, however, they were disappointed. The changed electronic version did not meet the expectations that they associated with the brand's gameplay. It didn't have the brand consistency I or the consumer expected from the Phase 10 brand. So I forced the licensee to make the necessary changes to bring that product in line with the overall brand.

The consistency of the trademarked product, by the way, doesn't have to be the highest level of quality in a given industry. It just has to represent consistency of quality within the brand. When you buy a new Mercedes-Benz, for instance, you expect a level of quality that's different than that of a Honda Civic. But both brands offer a consistent level of quality the consumers expect as a result of their use of the respective products.

Importance of a Strong Brand

A trademark will apply to almost any invention that is a consumer product. You may not seek a patent, whether you're eligible for one or not. In fact, avoiding the patenting process may be inadvisable. A copyright may not apply to your particular product or invention.

A trademark, on the other hand, provided it is a consumer product that you've invented, will usually apply. You will seek a trademark so that people can have a way to identify the quality and consistency of your product. You want to come up with a catchy name for your trademark, for your product, so that it stands out from its competitors and is memorable.

You want to develop a trademark that is strong, one that is distinctive so that it won't be confused with a similar product in the same industry. So, if your toothbrush is called Brand X, you don't want your competitor to name their toothbrush Brand XY. People may not know exactly what they're getting. They may think XY comes from X, or X comes from XY, or they may think they're one and the same.

Don't rush through this important phase. Take whatever time you need to come up with a brand name that will clearly distinguish your product from its competitors in the eyes of your consumers. This is what I mean by a "strong" trademark; it is distinctive and distinguishable from all other brands.

Conclusion

The above is an overview of how the process works and why these forms of IP might be beneficial to you as an inventor. The nuts and bolts of how, why, when, where, and what applies specifically to your invention are beyond the scope of this book. However, I invite you to look at the videos on my website: www.thesimpleplan.com

Also, consult an attorney who can specifically advise you based on your particular product and circumstance.

Is IP Registration Necessary to Make MONEY?

One important fact that you must keep in mind: You don't need to register intellectual property to make a fortune from your invention. IP registration is not necessary or required for success. You don't have to own a patent; you don't have to register your copyright or trademark. You apply for one of the forms of IP to preclude others from copying or somehow utilizing your brand, your utility, and your product, in a way that competes with your invention. It is designed to give you exclusivity as it relates to your invention.

Some people believe that because they've obtained a patent they are ensured of success with their invention. After all, the government issued the patent after comparing it with other patent applications and other products in the public domain, and determined that it was unique and novel.

Even though the USPTO may issue you a patent, it does not mean the invention will be successful. There are tons of patented products out there. Some have made it to the marketplace; others haven't. *Most* have not earned a dime for their inventors. Over 90% of all patents issued to independent inventors have not earned enough money for the inventors to recover the cost of their patents.

Nevertheless, IP registration is wise provided it is sought at the right time in the process as you have learned in this book.

Chapter 13

Step 6 of The Simple Plan:

License/Venture

"Accept the challenges, so that you may feel the exhilaration of victory." General George S. Patton

"No problem can stand the assault of sustained thinking." Voltaire

Whether you're going to license your invention or venture your invention, this is where you make your money.

When you license your invention to a manufacturer, the manufacturer then promotes it and distributes it for you, while you earn a royalty on those sales. When you venture it, you begin a business, start a manufacturing operation to produce your product, get it out there onto the store shelves and into the public, and hopefully build a successful business.

In this chapter, I outline both of these options.

Part 1: Licensing

You've completed the first five steps of *The Simple Plan* and determined that you have a potentially successful invention. Now, do you license or venture? In the chapter title, I have a slash between the two terms because in most cases you're going to do either one or the other.

In some cases, you'll do both. You'll venture, then license, which is what I did for my products. But most inventors will license exclusively. That's the route I recommend for most inventors. I'll get into the reasons why as we move forward in this chapter. So, let's jump into it. We'll start with the basics.

What Is a License?

A license is simply an agreement by which you, the licensor, allow someone else, the licensee, to commercially manufacture and distribute your invention for a period of time. In most cases, the license agreement will be in perpetuity, meaning that it will last indefinitely, provided the licensee meets certain hurdles and requirements, which we'll get into later.

When you license, you are essentially leasing your legal rights, much like a person who owns a house. If you want to rent or lease your house to someone, you have that person sign a lease agreement. That agreement entitles the person to use your house for whatever period of time you've agreed to. In exchange for the right to use your property, the person must pay you rent.

The license of your intellectual property, your invention, works the same way, though the payment you receive is called a royalty. You are essentially leasing your legal rights to the licensee to manufacture and distribute your invention; in exchange, the licensee will pay you a royalty, which usually is a percentage of the wholesale price of the invention.

Key Elements of a License Agreement

Below are key elements of a license agreement.

Remember this: Licenses can be very flexible and *every clause in the agreement is negotiable*.

Term

The term is how long the agreement lasts. Typically, a licensee will want the term to last indefinitely. As the inventor, you may not like this but the request is common. Most licensees will not agree to build a product's presence in the marketplace only to lose the license in a few years. So, more important to you than the term is that they meet certain hurdles, such as they produce or they sell X number of units per year, or they achieve a certain sales volume per year, or you're guaranteed to receive a minimum royalty dollar amount per year, in exchange for the perpetual term.

Royalty Rate

There is no standard rate that applies in every case. While in most industries there is an average rate that falls within a specific range, your specific royalty rate is negotiable and depends on a lot of variables and circumstances. (For more on royalty rate, see below.) Even what seems like a low royalty rate can bring you a big check.

For instance, if XYZ Company, the licensee, agrees to sell your widget at a wholesale level of $10, and your royalty agreement stipulates that you earn 5% of that $10, then you'll earn $0.50 for every unit they sell. If the wholesale price of your widget is $100, then you will earn $5 for every unit they sell.

Now, $0.50 or $5 may not sound like much, but if, for instance, your product sells $1 million worth of units at wholesale per year and you have a royalty rate of 5%, you earn $50,000 in passive income per year.

That's a pretty good income for just going to your mailbox, picking up your check, and taking it to the bank. If your invention sells $10 million at wholesale, a 5% royalty will yield you $500,000 per year in passive income! WOW!

Guaranteed Annual Minimum Royalty

Typically a license agreement will stipulate exactly what the inventor's guaranteed annual minimum royalty (GAMR) will be. It is stated in the form of a dollar amount. For example, if the contract stipulates that the GAMR is $50,000, then XYZ Company, the licensee, will guarantee that your royalty in any year will be a minimum of $50,000 regardless of what their sales are for that year. If they don't pay that minimum amount, then you can move to terminate the license.

Exclusive or Non-Exclusive License

Typically, a licensee will want an exclusive worldwide deal for at least two reasons: 1) They will not want to compete against someone else in the same space; and 2) Without an exclusive they will lack complete control over the brand and quality of products made by other licensees.

But you don't have to give them such broad rights. Sometimes you can give them an exclusive deal based on a limited geographic range or location. So, for instance, you could give one company an exclusive right to manufacture and distribute the product in all of North America while you may grant another company a license of those same rights for the rest of the world.

Or the deal may be based on specific distribution channels or applications of the invention. As an example, you might allow one licensee to be an exclusive distributor to "big box" retailers, while another licensee has the exclusive right to distribute to "specialty" retailers or all other retailers.

One licensee could have rights to e-commerce, while another could be granted a license to distribute to "brick and mortar" retailers.

Application rights can be broken down in various ways as well. If your invention has industrial use, you can break down the right to distribute according to industry: for example, automotive, aerospace, chemical, pharmaceutical, or consumer products.

Or you can offer licenses based on geography. I've done this, offered exclusive licenses broken down to individual segments of the market. At one point I had a licensee with exclusive rights to the world except Europe. A different licensee had the exclusive rights to Europe. A third licensee had an exclusive right to digital products including mobile applications.

Most licensees will want an exclusive license worldwide in all channels and industries. So you will have to determine if the deal they offer makes sense to you. Just because a licensee wants an exclusive agreement doesn't mean you have to grant it.

If they have a strong distribution presence worldwide, you might consider giving them worldwide rights. However, most will not have that kind of presence. They will usually distribute the product in the marketplace where they have a presence and then "sub-license" to others with presence elsewhere. In a sub-license arrangement, your licensee will offer a sub-license to a third party and collect royalties based upon their sales, then split the royalty with you on a 50/50 or 60/40 basis.

IP Ownership and Maintenance

As the licensor, when you license your invention to a licensee, you are not generally giving away ownership of your intellectual property (IP). You are simply leasing certain rights that ownership gives you, most notably the rights to manufacture and distribute. This is how I have always done it with my games. I do not "sell" the IP. I simply license the distribution and manufacturing rights.

In some cases, you may give a complete assignment, which means that you are actually transferring your right of *ownership* of the IP to your licensee, whether that ownership is through a patent, a copyright, or a trademark. The licensee now owns the intellectual property and controls the rights that you formerly had to distribute, manufacture, and do whatever else they want to do with it as long as they pay you whatever royalty or lump sum you've negotiated with them.

Licensing Pros and Cons

As with most anything, licensing, too, has its own set of pros and cons. What are the pros and cons of licensing? Let's look at them.

The Cons

You lose control of the technology

Once you give a license to someone to manufacture and distribute your invention, you basically lose control of it.

There are ways to maintain some control. You can put in place an approval requirement for any changes or adjustments the licensee may make. But, generally speaking, you will lose control. You just have to be prepared for this outcome. There's nothing wrong with giving up control as long as you understand, going into the deal, what control you're going to maintain and what control you're going to give up, and both parties agree upon it.

Your own involvement is reduced

Obviously once you have a licensee, your licensee is going to be involved in the day-to-day situations related to the product while you sit back and collect royalties. There's nothing wrong with this, again, as long as you understand that your involvement will be greatly reduced.

Finding the right licensee can be tough

In most industries, finding a licensee is not very difficult. If you develop a consumer product that will sit on a shelf in a retail store somewhere, you'll find that there will be one or more competing products on the same shelf that were designed to resolve the same problem that your product resolves. Oftentimes, your prospective licensee will be a company that is making one of those products.

However, in cases where you develop new technology, a licensee is not so readily apparent. This is when it becomes difficult. (For more on finding a licensee, see below.)

Protecting your interest is crucial ... and extremely difficult

Part 2 - The Simple Plan

This is when a good attorney is helpful. The attorney can help you negotiate the license deal in the first place so that your interests are protected. Then you have to stay on top of the licensee. You can do this by staying in touch with someone who works for the licensee. Companies that work with a lot of inventors likely will have someone in charge of inventor relations. Contact the appropriate person at least once a year just to see what is going on and what future plans they may have or are developing for your invention. Check out stores where it is being sold from time to time so you can see how well it is selling and so you can monitor any changes to the packaging.

Breaches of the License Agreement

A licensee will oftentimes breach immaterial sections of the contract, meaning those sections that are viewed as not critical to the overall agreement. Usually those breaches occur by accident. For example, your licensee may have the habit of not sending you a royalty report on a timely basis per the agreement, or of not sending you a requested sample on time. These are considered small infractions and immaterial to the overall agreement. Still, when they occur, you should bring them to the licensee's attention and see to it that they comply ASAP.

Material breaches are those breaches that are central to the agreement. They include the most critical of all: not paying royalties! If your licensee does not pay all due royalties, they are in the most serious form of a breach possible under a license agreement.

Remember, bring all breaches to the attention of the licensee.

The Pros

A licensee with resources

Licensing multiplies the resources to develop your invention. Instead of you being there in your basement, developing your invention, and trying to get it on the market, you now have a licensee who, if you've chosen well, already has distribution in place. They have their own research and development (R&D) department to further develop your invention. They have brand recognition in the marketplace, a customer base, and, of course, the ability to manufacture the product.

Additional uses and markets

158

Chapter 13 - Step 6 of The Simple Plan: License/Venture

Licensees often see uses and markets you do not see or have access to. They know what the trends are in the industry. If you followed step one of *The Simple Plan*, research evaluation, you now have a better grasp of the trends in the industry as well. But they know them better. They're in the trenches every day, and they will likely have greater insight than you.

Upfront money

The licensee may pay you money upfront. This doesn't happen all the time, but it does happen on occasion. That payment may be in a form of an advance against future royalties. Or it may actually be an upfront payment, essentially a reimbursement for some of the development or IP costs that you have incurred.

This is particularly true if you ventured the invention before licensing it. In that case, you have developed the market for it. You've already got it in retail. You've saved them a lot of work and effort to launch it, so you can demand an upfront payment that is not a part of an advance against royalties. It's simply a cash payment.

Phase 10 had been on the market for many years when I starting licensing it. I had already developed a relationship with Kmart, which at that time was the largest retailer in the country. So it was easy to ask for an upfront cash payment, just for signing the license deal.

An advance doesn't happen all the time but it could. However, *don't* hold out and develop the "greedy inventor syndrome," which causes you to make unreasonable demands that threaten or ruin a potential license deal. "Upfront money" will likely only happen if

- You have proven the product will sell by actually selling a few thousand in the marketplace.

- You are being reimbursed for IP expenses.

- You are selling inventory to the licensee or manufacturing equipment.

So only ask for some kind of payment when it is appropriate and you've gauged the willingness of your licensee. Remember, everything is negotiable. If you can negotiate an upfront fee, great! If you can't, you must consider whether to walk away and go with a licensee that will give you an upfront fee or take the deal without an upfront fee. But don't blow the deal if you don't have alternative licensees waiting.

Licensing allows you to be free for other pursuits

Licensing can be an advantage to you when you want to be free from venturing. A license gives you the freedom to pursue other inventions, other interests in your life, or other business opportunities. You can do whatever you want because you are not tied to the day-to-day operation and development of your invention. And all the while you can receive royalty checks.

Most inventors like the opportunity to have freedom – particularly if they make enough money from royalties that they don't have to do anything else for a living. They can sit back, collect royalties, and pursue their life's dreams.

Three Pre-Licensing Concerns

When they are first beginning to think about the possibility of licensing, inventors seem most concerned about three issues:

- royalty rate
- upfront money
- invention commercialization

Royalty Rate

One of the most common questions I hear is, "What is my royalty rate going to be?"

The answer typically depends on the industry. Every industry has a royalty range. It could be 2% to 4%. It could be 3% to 5%. It could be 5% to 8%. This is where your contact with the industry association, your attendance at trade shows, and your practice of just talking to potential licensees will help you determine what to expect as a range of royalties in your invention's industry.

You can then determine for yourself if your desired rate falls within the range and how you can get it there if it doesn't. Sometimes you'll be at the low end or the high end of the range. Oftentimes, the ranges are dictated by product cost and profit margin. A number of factors will determine where you fall in the royalty range of your industry. But again, do your homework.

Upfront Money

Another of the most-asked questions I hear is, "How much upfront money will I receive?" Answers to this question are all over the map. As I wrote earlier, an upfront payment could be any amount, depending mainly on how far along you are in developing and marketing your invention. What I mean by upfront money here is a payment that is not an advance against future royalties. *In most cases, however, there is no upfront money!*

Invention Commercialization

"How can I keep the company from sitting on my idea and not doing anything to commercialize it?"

The *guaranteed annual minimum royalty* (GAMR) that you negotiated into your license agreement should determine your answer. By means of the GAMR, the licensee will be required to pay you a specified minimum annual amount, whether or not they've actually achieved sales to justify that amount. Since they are required to pay that minimum amount regardless of the actual sales volume, your licensee will want to keep the product moving so that they don't have to dig into their pockets to pay you money that has not been earned.

So the GAMR keeps them motivated to commercialize your invention and actively market it. If, in fact, they don't achieve those minimums, you usually have the right to terminate the agreement, take the product, and seek out a new licensee.

The amount of the GAMR is something you will negotiate into the license agreement. Here again you must be reasonable in the GAMR amount you request. If you ask for a GAMR that is too high you will likely be faced with pushback and a potential deal breaker.

Finding a Licensee

Now that you know what a license is and its important elements, how do you find potential licensee targets? The first places to check are the stores and the Internet.

At stores, you simply go down the aisle that's appropriate for your invention.

If you've created a new comb, for instance, then you go down the aisle where other combs are waiting to be sold, look at their packages, and write down the manufacturers' names. Note any other information that you find out about them, including where they are located. Take a look at their website and Google them for more info about their products and the company in general. Also, try to determine what else they manufacture, and look for any interesting historical tidbits that you can find about the company.

You can also find licensees on the Internet. Search using not store aisles but Google and keywords associated with your invention.

Now that you've found licensing targets, again, learn as much as you can about each of them. Check out their websites and those of their competitors. Go to the store and look at all of their products. If they are a public company, see how much money they are making and review their annual reports. Talk to retailers about the products in the company's product line.

Prioritize your potential licensees based on their perceived likelihood and/ or interest in licensing. Have they done such a license deal in the past?

It is important to know also if your product fits into their product line. If a target does not make combs and your product is a comb, then you don't want to talk to them. If they make combs and distribute them, then you should consider them as a possible target.

If you've developed a new vacuum cleaner for home use, you may want to contact Hoover and Dyson, to see if they want to license your technology but you should not approach General Motors.

Find as much information as you can about each target company before you contact them so that on the day of your meeting you can walk into their offices knowing who they are and how they do business. Your knowledge of the company will impress them. But beyond that, you want to fully understand the company you are dealing with as a potential licensee.

Is the Target Company Interested in Licensing?

In your initial conversation with your potential licensee, you want to find out if they consider products "created on the outside" for license deals. Some companies definitely *will not* look at products that are not created inside their company. Others will, but they will only work through brokers, not with individual inventors.

Still others will be happy to look at your product, and deal with you on an individual basis. This practice is absolutely acceptable to them. If you research diligently, you often will find companies that are so interested in licensing that on their website they will have a tab that provides instructions on how inventors can submit their ideas. That's certainly true in the game industry. It's true in a lot of other industries as well. Once you know which company or companies you want to go after, prepare an individualized licensing plan for each target.

Licensing Plan

The licensing plan should include the following information. Much of it you will already have if you completed the previous steps of *The Simple Plan*:

Your Background

Whatever your background is in your industry, mention it. If, for example, you've developed a new vacuum cleaner and you worked for Dyson or Hoover, or you have developed other vacuum cleaning products, tell them. These experiences give you credibility and show that you understand the business. If you don't have any experience to mention, it's not necessarily a negative; but if you do, it's definitely a positive.

Product Description

Your product description should describe your invention, its benefits, and how it works. What problem does it solve? Why did you feel the need to develop it?

Features

What special features make your product exceptional? Why is it better than its competitors?

Manufacturing Cost Estimates

How much will your product cost to manufacture? What will be its likely retail price? How do those figures compare? What is the profit margin?

In step three of *The Simple Plan*, you did the product evaluation. During that level of evaluation, you evaluated your prototype, you figured all the material needed to go into production, and you priced it out to determine what the manufacturing cost of your product would be.

Also, cost information can be easily obtained simply by going to individual contract manufacturers and asking them to give you prices based on various volumes. The volume production estimate could be based on 10,000, 50,000, or 100,000 units. With that estimate you now have a cost to manufacture. You can give that information to your prospective licensee. Sometimes they are able to produce it for less than your estimate, but your estimate gives them an initial idea, a starting point.

Materials List

You compiled your materials list during your product evaluation of the prototype.

Market Size

You determined market size in the first step of *The Simple Plan* when you did the market research.

Existing Competition

List the existing competing products. Who is the manufacturer of each one? What are its features and benefits? What is its retail price? What is its market share? If you can't get all of this information, don't worry. But if you have it, include it. Gather as much information on the competing products as you can so that you can present a comprehensive, side-by-side comparison of the respective competitors to your product. By doing this, hopefully you will be able to show why your invention is superior to the competing products.

Market Drivers and Trends

What's the main driver in the marketplace for your invention? What forces are driving that trend? This information you will learn through the industry association, the one you joined, or at least spoke to, while doing step one of *The Simple Plan*, the research evaluation, or step three, the product evaluation.

Proof the Product Will Sell

If you've accumulated sales data through customer surveys or if you've actually sold some of the product, then this is proof that it will sell. If you have such evidence, you certainly want to present it.

Chapter 13 - Step 6 of The Simple Plan: License/Venture

Positioning Strategy

The positioning strategy of your product should answer the following questions:

- How is it better than the other products?
- What benefits and features make it better?
- How will it be priced relative to competing products in the marketplace?

Target Customer

Who is your target customer? You have to really think about this answer and be specific. You can't just say, if you have a new comb, "It's for everyone who has hair." If it was designed to "detangle hair better than any other comb," you say it's for people who have problems with tangled hair. That's your target customer. It's not for everyone who uses a comb.

Your packaging and promotion will all focus on how well it detangles hair.

Is Your Invention Fully Developed?

If your invention is fully developed, mention that fact in the plan. If it needs further development or tweaking, mention that also, along with what you think needs to be done to fully develop it.

Further Development Requirements

If needed, what else must be done to prepare the invention for the market? Are you in a position to help with this further development? How much will it cost to finish the development?

Timetable

If your product is fully developed and ready now, make that clear. If it needs more development, say how much development it needs and give as accurate an estimate as you can for when it will be ready to be introduced to the market.

Is It Seasonal?

In what season is your product used: winter, summer, spring, or fall? Seasonal products will have limitations and regional appeal. What are they?

Part 2 - The Simple Plan

Presenting to Potential Licensees

You've selected your target potential licensees. You've written a licensing plan for each target. The information from each licensing plan will be used to organize your presentation. Now, it's time to make your presentation.

The product demonstration part of the presentation, when possible, should be done live. However, some products should be demonstrated via a video demonstration of the product in use. For particularly large products, you will want to have a video showing the product in use, along with photographs and other visuals.

Begin with Brief Overview

For the overview, you draw information from your licensing plan. The overview should provide information such as:

- a brief product description
- the target market
- market size
- annual sales and gross profit potential (you should have learned this from your market research and the product evaluation)

Take a minute or two, just long enough to hit on each of these points.

State Why You Developed the Product

Why did you develop the product in the first place? What problem does it solve?

Verify the Product's Need

Verify that the market sees the same need for the product as you do by showing the results of questionnaires, focus groups, and surveys. If you have made sales of the product, provide actual sales results. How recurring is the problem that your product resolves? How do consumers resolve it now? What would they pay? Do they like using your prototype? Why?

Design Objectives

What problem is your invention designed to solve? How does it work? How effectively and efficiently does it resolve the problem?

Chapter 13 - Step 6 of The Simple Plan: License/Venture

Show and Demonstrate

After providing your oral presentation about your product, now it's time to demonstrate it. Show them what it is and how it does what it does. At this time, you will list the major selling features and benefits of the product.

Provide Manufacturing Cost Estimates

After the demonstration, lay out the projected manufacturing costs in detail. If it feels better to you, you can provide this information before the demonstration.

Timetable

Finally, present your introduction timetable. When would or should you/ they introduce it into the marketplace?

Offer Ongoing Support

After you've shared your licensing plan, demonstrated your product, talked about its benefits and features, and given them your timetable, offer them any additional support they may need to further develop it, if it needs further developing, or to help in the launch and ongoing promotion. Make sure you let them know that you are there to help.

Wrap Up the Meeting

And then you'll wrap up the meeting by thanking them for their time and attention.

You're done! You've completed the presentation. You've provided survey results and sales statistics that prove that it will sell. You've shown them the market. You've given them cost and profit estimates. You've done your best to educate them on the license-worthiness of your invention/ product. Now it's time to negotiate the license deal. Hopefully they are excited and want to do a deal with you.

Now, It's Time to Negotiate

All license agreements contain the same basic elements, or should. The exact terms of those elements differ from contract to contract. Remember, everything is negotiable! Below are a few of the major terms.

Part 2 - The Simple Plan

Nature of the License

Is it exclusive or non-exclusive? Exclusive mean they are the only licensee for a given geography, medium, or category. Non-exclusive means they are not the only licensee.

Definition of What Is Being Licensed

You must define exactly what IP you're licensing. That may sound simple, but you have to spell this out in the contract. For registered IP, note in the agreement appropriate file or registration numbers. For example, if you have an issued patent, the license agreement should note the patent number and exhibit the patent itself as an exhibit item.

Geography or Market Limitations

Whether you're going to give them an exclusive license for North America or an exclusive license for the world should be spelled out. You can give them an exclusive license for the world but reserve the right to license the technology for app development for mobile devices to another party. That is an example of market limitations that you may implement or include in your license agreement.

Future Inventions or Brand Extensions

Did you give the licensee the right to make extensions or future inventions off your technology? If so, how will you be paid? How much will you be paid? When will you be paid? Who will own those improvements, brand extensions, and spinoff products?

Term and Termination

For what length of time will the agreement last and how will it be terminated?

Right to Audit

You'll definitely want the right to audit their books and records. This provision allows you to make sure you're being paid what you should be paid.

However, your licensee is not going to want you coming in every six months to audit their books, and with good reason: They don't want the disruption to their operations. So, typically an agreement will give you the right to audit every year or every two years.

Also, you will typically have a window of time within which to perform the audit. For example, during the first ninety days of the new year, you will have a right to audit the books of the previous year. Or the window might be from June through September because your licensee may not want non-employees in their offices during their busy season.

The audit clause should indicate the number of years in the past you have a right to audit. For instance, if your contract says you can audit books for any time period going back five years, you can't look at their books from six years ago.

Licensees want this right to limit the historical timeframe because they may not want to hold onto books and records forever just so that you can audit them whenever you want. This way, at the end of that timeframe, they can dispose of their books and records or put them in storage somewhere and not worry about their being easily accessible for your benefit.

So don't be spooked if they say, "We only want you to be able to go back five years." If you know that going in, then just get your audits done, if you desire to perform an audit, before the deadline. If you think audits will be necessary, get them done as frequently as you're allowed, so that you don't have to worry about missing the deadline.

Regarding responsibility for payment of the audit, it is common for the licensor, you, to take on this responsibility. However, it is also common to add a clause to the agreement allowing you to require the licensee to pay for the audit if the audit shows an under payment exceeding some percent of the overall payment due.

So, in this case, if there is an under payment exceeding the threshold, the licensee will be required to pay for the audit. Of course, all of this is negotiable.

Patent Expense

If you have NOT yet applied for a patent or it is still pending, who's going to pay for the initial application and/or ongoing cost? Many times inventors will request that the licensee pay for it and, of course, name the licensor, you, the inventor, as the creator/author/inventor of the product. As the inventor, you must be named as such in the patent application regardless of who is paying for it. The same is true for copyright registration: You must be named as the author.

Infringement by Others

If an infringement is determined or recognized, who pays for the litigation? Usually the licensee will pay for any litigation at no cost to the licensor, you. However, sometimes the licensee will expect you to likewise be on the lookout for infringement and bring any that you spot to their attention.

Right to Sub-license

So, your licensee gives a license to someone else, maybe to cover a geographic area or a specific market segment where they're not adept or don't have distribution. For instance, your licensee has the right to market your product throughout the whole world, but they sub-license to someone in Europe or Asia.

Do they have the right to do that? That is determined in the agreement. Typically, if you do give them the right to sub-license, you will want them to give you the right to review any agreement that they strike and to sign off on it. In exchange, you will assure them that your approval will not be unreasonably withheld. So, it's not bad to allow them to sub-license. However you do want the right to know who those sub-licensees are and to review their agreement.

Also, you must agree upon a split of the royalties proceeding from the sub-licensee's sales. A split of 50/50 or 60/40 is common. However, your industry may vary from this split model. A variation from the above norm may also arise in cases where your direct licensee has financial risk associated with the sub-licensee's efforts.

Patent or Other IP Assignment

Are you assigning the patent or other intellectual property or not? This should be spelled out in the agreement. You are making an assignment when you sign over your IP *ownership* to another party. Sometimes licensees insist on this as part of the license. I personally prefer to maintain IP ownership. However, an assignment is not necessarily bad if you have negotiated all the other provisions in your agreement to your liking.

5 "Don'ts" When Negotiating

Negotiating is often treated as an adversarial confrontation between two opposing sides but the negotiation and outcome needn't be adversarial at all. In fact, once you sign your licensing agreement, you want to view your licensee as your partner in the success of your product. True partnership is earned over time through trust and cooperation. You'll get there faster if you avoid the 5 "Don'ts" when negotiating:

1. Don't have unrealistic expectations. I've seen this a lot. Inventors expect the world from the licensee, and it's just out of the realm of possibility. Maybe the inventor is asking for way too much upfront money. Whatever the case, don't be unrealistic.

2. Don't bluff. I've seen inventors try to bluff their way into a deal. Some act like they're going to storm out of the room if they don't get the terms they want. Don't do that. Don't be a bully. Just negotiate realistically and fairly. You want to build a strong relationship with your licensee, not an adversarial one. Okay? So work with them and be reasonable. Make them your advocate and you'll both be rewarded for the good relationship.

3. Don't continue negotiating after you've already agreed on terms. Know when to quit. You may negotiate yourself right out of a deal.

4. Don't ask for an exorbitant amount of money when you're willing to settle for a fraction of it. If you know you are willing to settle for an amount, don't get ridiculous and ask for the moon because you'll blow the deal. I can't tell you the number of times I've seen deals blown out of greed.

5. Don't reject an offer today if you can put off that rejection until tomorrow. In other words, if you think you're going to reject an offer, sleep on it, think about it, and figure out what's bothering you. Then come up with ideas on how to improve it so that you can negotiate tomorrow. If, when tomorrow comes, you still want to reject the offer, then reject the offer. But sleep on it first.

Conclusion

Licensing, for most inventors, is the best method to commercialize their inventions. As a rule, most inventors simply do not have the operations, manufacturing, financial resources, and marketing experience necessary for successful venturing.

Licensing also is far less risky than venturing. Finding a qualified licensee takes homework and persistence, but, whatever you spend trying to find your licensee, venturing will cost you far, far more.

For these reasons, licensing is the best path for most of you out there. Venturing is a great path also, but it's not for everyone. Find out if it's for you in the next half of this chapter.

Part 2: Venturing

In the first half of this chapter, I talked about licensing. For those inventors with little to no cash reserves, experience, or risk tolerance, it's the way to go. However, in this half of the chapter, I introduce you to the venturing strategy.

Starting a business, or venturing, as it's often called, will require more from you. To begin with, *venturing requires much more work!* If you want to make your business a success, you must devote your time and your resources to doing whatever it takes to get your invention into the marketplace. You must be prepared for that.

Some of you may say, "Well, I still want to have a company. I want to build my own business." I was like that, too. I didn't get into the game business to license, although that's what I did with my first game, Dice Baseball. But with Phase 10, my second game, I became a publisher (sometimes game manufacturers are referred to as "publisher"). I got into the venturing side.

Besides the advantages that come with being your own boss, venturing provides some real advantages for later licensing or for sale of the business. I'll talk more about advantages of venturing below. But first, let's look at the disadvantages.

Venturing Disadvantages
Most New Businesses Fail

A new business built around a single new product runs a double risk, especially since the list of reasons for business failures reads like a catalog of inventors' weaknesses. Many inventors, like your average person out there, don't have the temperament, the capital resources, or the skills required to operate a business successfully. Not every inventor will suffer from these common disadvantages, but many do.

Licensing is less risky. It doesn't require capital resources or the management skills that are required to operate a business successfully. However, if you want to pursue a business, you must look at the risks, and there are many.

Inadequate Financing

A lot of inventors who want to pursue a business for their invention find that they don't have the financing to launch their product. Launching a new product can be costly. If you have never started a business before, you will add to your financial risk due to your lack of experience.

Lack of Management Skills

Inventors who venture must manage:

- personnel
- production
- accounting
- marketing
- sales

Can you do all that while still allowing your creative mind to invent new products? Many inventors can't and that's okay if they stick to licensing.

Overestimating the Market

Sometimes – in fact, probably most of the time – I've seen inventors think that everyone on Earth is going to want their product. They've overestimated the demand for their product in the marketplace. The reality that they encounter is quite different from the reality they have estimated.

Poor Choice of Location

You've heard the expression, "Location, location, location." If your business requires a retail location, then your chosen location for the business will be important. Do you have experience choosing business locations? If not, you will have to hire someone to help you.

Inability to Delegate Responsibility

Entrepreneurs often want to wear all the hats in their business. Sometimes they feel they have no other choice. Others are simply "control freaks." Whatever the case, you must delegate to be successful.

Remember, you're only one person. You only have so much time and energy. Pay others to do the day-to-day maintenance work so you can work on the big picture. Also, while you have your own skill sets, let's face it, everyone has some skills but no one has every skill. You must take advantage of the skills of others. Find those who excel where you don't.

Limited Resources

Finances are only one form of resources that might be limited. There are others. For instance, you need the knowledge and experience that it takes to operate a business. Also, contacts and mentors are helpful resources to grow and sustain your business. These may be limited for you, especially when you are starting out. You'll be spread increasingly thin. As you grow, your responsibilities will increase and become unbearable if you don't delegate.

You Probably Won't Make Much Money for Quite a While

Most businesses don't start making money on day one. It may take you years before your business is actually profitable. You have to plan ahead, put together your strategy, and calculate your financial projections so that you understand at what level of sales your break-even point will be. You must plan to survive without an income for a period of time.

Venturing Advantages

Venturing gives you the advantages that come with being your own boss while also putting you in a good position if you later want to get into licensing your product or selling your business. By venturing you can "prove" that your invention will sell in the marketplace, that consumers want it, and that you've got a track record of selling it. You can negotiate a far more favorable license deal if you've already done a successful venture of your invention. Following are a few advantages of venturing.

Running a Company Can Be Exciting

"Exhilarating" may be a better word. You will derive a lot of satisfaction from growing your business and seeing your efforts make it successful.

In the Long Run You May Make a Lot of Money

Assuming you survive the difficult period in the beginning, you stand to make a lot more money as a business owner who is venturing your invention than you would as a licensee. This assumes your invention as a product will have good margins and you run a lean, efficient operation.

Early on you will not be profitable as you build the business and reinvest profits into the operation. Eventually, though, you will be able to draw profits and, after all is said and done, you should make more than the royalty percentage you would otherwise receive as a licensor.

Even Though It's Your Company, You May Not Have to Run It

You can own a company and not be there running it day to day. This won't happen in the beginning when everything is new and your attention is needed everywhere to get it off the ground. But if all goes well and it grows as a healthy business, there will come a time when you can delegate day-to-day management functions to others. Again, it's not likely to happen at the beginning but it will happen.

Required Phases for Successful Business Management

Successful management of a business requires that you complete three phases:

1. Launching the business
2. Mastering what you're doing and the business operation
3. Controlling a dynamic process

Your business is growing, it's dynamic and fluid, and you have a lot to learn. You'll be dealing with continuous changes caused by business growth, new technology in the industry, revisions to tax laws, the behavior of your competition, and other factors. These factors are dynamic and fluid as well. You'll have to stay on top of them. As a successful manager, you must control or stay on top of the dynamic process of change and evolution that occurs in operating a business.

Prerequisites to Venturing

Before you begin your venturing operation, this is what you need:

Part 2 - The Simple Plan

Proof That the Invention Works

If you built and tested your prototype, you should already know if it works or not and, if it didn't, what you had to do to make it work. Before you try venturing, you must make certain that your invention performs the function for which it was created, and it does so effectively and efficiently in such a way that its benefits outweigh the benefits of the competition.

Market Analysis

This goes back to step one of *The Simple Plan*. You should have done a thorough market analysis. You should know who your customers are, how to find them, what your target is, what they will pay, and the distribution channel through which your products may be purchased.

Commercialization Plan

Your business plan encompasses:

- marketing plan
- management staff
- financial projections
- distribution strategy
- who you're going to pursue as distributors and retailers

No matter which commercialization strategy you follow, you will increasingly have to involve yourself with people from the business world. If you are not now in the business world, it will be a whole new world for you. You must learn how to deal with their various attitudes and personalities. This is not a negative, just something you need to understand.

You'll deal with a lot of different people. They will hold different views and have different expectations. They may speak a different language or use industry jargon with which you are not currently familiar. So you will need to learn the terminology, the technology, and the differences in attitude and expectations of each person you meet.

As the inventor, you are excited about your product. You have the vision, the goal to get it into the marketplace. The people around you, those with whom you are doing business, only look at it as a potential moneymaker.

They do not share your long-term and maybe emotional attachment to the product. You have to face that reality and learn how to deal with these people pretty much on their terms because, like it or not, you will increasingly need them.

Use Elements of the Licensing Plan to Build Your Business Plan

Use the elements of the licensing plan that we spoke about earlier in this chapter to help you plan and prepare your business plan. Those elements include any proof of sales, your markets, the overall market, your customers and how you're going to target them, surveys, retailers you plan to target, and other information that you have compiled to build out your licensing strategy.

Here are some of the key elements:

Market Research

You did this research in the first step of *The Simple Plan*. Now roll it into your business plan. Your former licensing plan is basically a business plan now.

Manufacturing Issues

How much will the manufacturing of your invention cost? What materials will be necessary? Will you assemble and manufacture the product or will you hire contract manufacturers to handle any or all of those tasks?

When I started my card game business, I would buy the custom card decks, the boxes, the instructions, and other packaging components from contract manufacturers. They made the components to my specifications. The components were then shipped to my factory (which initially was my parents' basement). Then my team, my friends and family members, would assemble the games and prepare them for shipment to customers.

How will you manufacture your product?

Competition Issues

You learned about your competition by following steps one and three of *The Simple Plan*. Your plan should demonstrate how your product is better and how well it will be able to stand up to competing products

Part 2 - The Simple Plan

Operational Issues

Who's going to handle the various roles of your business operations? How is payroll going to look? What days of the week are you going to work, and what hours? If you're going to do assembly work, where will you find the workers? How are you going to compensate them? What benefits will you provide, if any? Marketing, distribution, and sales: How will they look?

Early on, you might consider outsourcing for your payroll and HR functions to firms that specialize in performing these tasks. Paychex is a well-known national firm well positioned to help in this regard.

When I first started my game assembly work, I hired temporary workers, friends, and family for this work. As my business grew, I continued to use temps until I reached the point of needing full-time assembly workers.

To help with marketing and sales, during this early stage of your business, you might consider hiring manufacturers' and/or sales reps. Good reps are an invaluable asset to your business, and they will usually work on a commission basis.

These are just some options you might consider using in the startup phase of your business. Because most work is on an as-needed or commission basis, you can keep your fixed operating costs low as you develop your early stage operation.

Funding Issues

Okay, here's the big one. How are you going to fund this whole adventure? Are you going to use your funds? Will you borrow money from a bank? Can you secure loans from friends and family?

Let's look at those financing options and a few others:

> • *Using your own funds.* When I started venturing Phase 10, I used my own money, until it ran out. Then I had to figure out other ways to obtain the cash I needed to sustain the business. You, too, can use your own funds to start out. You'll be better able to find lenders or investors later if they see you've already invested in the venture by using your own money.

> • *Securing loans from friends and family.* Most new businesses are funded by the founder – you – and friends and family. Since they

178

know you, these people can be a good source of funds, assuming they like your invention and believe you have a good plan to commercialize it.

• *Selling stock in the business.* When you sell stock in the business, you then have equity shareholders, people who invest in your business in exchange for a percentage of the business.

• *Bank financing.* Bank financing could come in the form of a second mortgage on your home or a loan against cash reserves you have in the bank. Since you are likely starting a new business with the venturing of your invention, a bank likely will NOT lend you money based on performance of the business because there has been no performance. Therefore, initial bank financing will use your personal credit, your personal history, and your personal assets as collateral.

• *Bringing on a partner.* The option of bringing on a partner is similar to selling stock, which I discussed above. But they aren't the same. When you sell stock, whether to one person or many, they become shareholders but they have no actual operational dealings with the business. A partner, on the other hand, invests in the business and then works with you to make it a success. You may have more than one partner. Vested partners can be a big help to you not only for their financial investment but because they may have skills and abilities that you don't have and that you need.

• *Angel investors.* Angel investors are oftentimes high-net-worth individuals who can fund your needs. When I discussed selling stock, I was thinking more of individual investors, usually friends or family, who give you smaller amounts, like $10,000, $20,000, or $50,000. If you can get enough of these people together, you can accumulate the total amount you need. The angel investor is usually someone you previously did not know who gives you the $50,000, $100,000, or more of cash you need to launch the business.

Manufacturing: You Can Do It Yourself

How do you get your invention manufactured? You can literally start your own manufacturing operation and do it yourself (DIY).

Part 2 - The Simple Plan

The way most inventors launch their businesses, however, is by using contract manufacturers.

I've talked about how I hired contract manufacturers to make the components of my games. I then gathered the components and assembled the games and prepared them for shipment in my warehouse. Automobile manufacturers like General Motors do not make every part of their cars either. Rather, they hire contract manufacturers to make car components and then GM assembles the cars. GM is considered the manufacturer of their cars, as I was the manufacturer or publisher of my card games, even though many of the components were actually made by other companies.

That's true with airplanes as well. In fact, it's true of many products that you buy from all industries. The company hires contract manufacturers to make the component parts and then they assemble them. Sometimes they even hire other companies to assemble them. In all cases, the primary company is still the manufacturer.

If you can't make the product yourself because it's too complex or the cost of the machinery to make it is too expensive, consider hiring someone else who already has those assets in place. The contract manufacturer simply charges you to make exactly the number of units you need.

Locating Potential Contract Manufacturers

There are many ways to locate potential contract manufacturers. Following are a few of them:

The Internet

Use keyword searching to find potential contract manufacturers on the Internet. For instance, if you need a widget manufacturer, then you do an Internet search using "widget manufacturers" (in quotes to search the term) as a keyword and you will find companies that make widgets. Use additional keywords to search by, for instance, geographical location.

Trade Shows and Associations

Go to the trade show or association that is appropriate for your invention and ask them about contract manufacturers for various components. Sometimes they will have a list of companies that are happy to make components or even the complete product for you.

Competitors

Believe it or not, manufacturers will oftentimes make products for their competition. In this way, they still create products out of their factories and they are able to operate their plants at greater capacity. Plus, they may eventually become your licensee through the process of the relationship.

Offshore Agents

A Google search will help you find offshore agents. If you can find one that is appropriate for your particular industry, they can help you find contract manufacturers in Europe, China, Southeast Asia, or anywhere else around the globe. In exchange for a fee, they will set up the arrangement and make sure that everything runs smoothly.

Set Up Your Distribution

Congratulations. You've set up the operation to manufacture your product, whether you are doing it yourself or with the help of a contractor. Now what? Time to set up your distribution network. Consider the following strategies:

Attend Industry Trade Shows

Go to industry trade shows. Usually in attendance are buyers of that industry from many of the retailers. The bigger the trade show, the more likely important retail buyers will attend.

For instance, in the toy industry, the big trade show is the Toy Fair, which is held in New York City every February. Manufacturers from around the world go there to display their new products, their new games, their new designs, their new packages, and their new toys. Buyers from the big retailers like Walmart and Target as well as from smaller retailers come to look for new products to display on their shelves. Many of them will give you orders right there, particularly the smaller retailers.

Others will set up appointments for you to come to their offices to demonstrate your product and give them further information about it. At that point, they'll either place an order, assign it for further review, or decline.

Find Local Merchants to Test Market Your New Product

Learn whatever you can about the industry and the distribution chain from the smaller local merchants. Get to know the local "mom and pop" retailers, and ask them to buy a small quantity of your product. They'll usually be happy to talk to you and appreciate that you value their opinion.

The smaller they are, the more likely they will be willing to take a chance with it. Oftentimes, the small guys need new, fresh products that can't be bought at the big retailers. They can't compete with the major retailers on price. So, they look for items that are not generally found at bigger retailers. Their patrons come to them looking to find these unique items.

As the product sales grow with the smaller retailers, you now have an example of its retail sales success that you can show to the major retailers.

Sign up a Manufacturer or Sales Rep

You can meet manufacturers' and sales reps at trade shows. You can find others in trade publications. They'll be listed in the back somewhere, usually among the classified ads where they will advertise their services.

These people and companies will represent you and your product to retailers or buyers in exchange for a commission, which could be anywhere from 5% to 10% of whatever they sell. In addition, as industry insiders, they can give you inside information. They can tell you what your package lacks and how you can make improvements.

Your trade association can tell you about trade shows and trade publications in your industry.

Use Social Media Marketing

In today's environment, social media is indispensable as a sales and distribution outlet. Also, platforms like Facebook can be a great public relations aid. It will be helpful to your efforts to launch your product.

Set Up a Website

Your website could be just a promotional site, but you will more likely want to also sell products there, particularly early on. With a website you can build market presence, which will in turn help you build brand and product awareness and get people excited about what you are doing.

Some retailers will not be thrilled about your selling products on your own website. However, as long as you don't undercut them on price, especially now while you are still small, they will be okay with it. The major retailers will likely be more opposed to you selling on your website. Remember, it's all negotiable.

Design a Compelling "Sale Sheet"

A sale sheet is basically a flyer. It should depict your product in a photo, maybe from different angles. It should list its features and benefits. It should contain information for the buyers that includes

- how many units are in a shipping case
- the unit weight and case weight
- any UPC codes associated with it

Approach Online Retailers and Catalog Houses

In today's environment, catalog houses are often forgotten, but they are still a great resource to get your product distributed. Approach them as you would smaller retailers. They, too, are always looking for unique products that they can offer their customers.

Conclusion

Venturing can be a great strategy. It may be the best strategy for you. But you have to examine yourself, be realistic, and determine whether you really want to run a business.

Do you have the skills and ability to manage and launch the business? Do you have the financial resources to launch your product and then sustain it as its sales grow?

In time, you will be able to get money from banks to fund that growth. But early on, you're going to have to fund the growth out of your pocket, through friends and family, through angel investors, or by means of the other resources we talked about.

Venturing worked for me. It was the strategy I used to launch Phase 10 and other games and get them into the biggest retailer in the country at the time, Kmart. A few years later, I decided to license. Finding a licensee at that point was no problem because they were all happy to take on a license of a product that was already selling well and being distributed by the largest retailer.

183

Part 2 - The Simple Plan

So, one way to get a license deal is by starting with a venture and proving that it sells.

But bear in mind that, for most inventors, a venturing strategy is not the way to go. Many want to just invent and leave the business of manufacturing and distribution to the licensee. That was my choice after venturing for over seven years. I had new inventions I wanted to launch, and other businesses outside of inventing that needed my attention.

Licensing frees you up to pursue those other goals. Venturing does not, particularly early on. Later, as you grow the business, you may develop it to the point where you are not involved in the day-to-day operations.

* * *

In wrapping up here, I hope you have stepped through all six steps or will, and you are prepared to take action on each one. Some of these steps, like the prototype, will take time. I hope you're on the path to getting it built, tested, and evaluated. Get your IP registered if that's your choice, and then start looking for a licensee or figuring out your business plan for venturing, so you can get your invention into the marketplace.

You don't want to delay, because you don't want someone else, independently of you, to come up with the same or a better solution than yours. Move forward while the idea is new and hot, strike while you can, and get your product on the shelf.

Part 3:

Intellectual Property

Chapter 14

Patent

"Abraham Lincoln was great, not because he once lived in a cabin, but because his goals got him out of it." Unknown

"Chance favors the prepared mind." Louis Pasteur

It's natural to be concerned about someone stealing your invention. You've got too much invested in terms of time, effort, and perhaps money to sit back and allow someone else to claim the credit and make the money.

But how soon should you run to the patent office to apply for "protection"? What kind of patent should you seek? And how much protection does a patent actually give you?

In this chapter, we're going to discuss "protection" of your invention. I put the key word in quotes because "protection," as it relate to patents, is a false notion.

You as an inventor are concerned about protecting your idea from predators, from those who would "steal" it. It is a legitimate concern to make sure that your idea has as much intellectual property rights protection as possible. You are wise to take advantage of the IP laws as much as possible and as necessary. Although it isn't always necessary to register your IP, in some cases it is advisable.

But you should not get bogged down with fear and worry over protecting your invention. You certainly should not run to the patent office as your first step.

Patent Basics

In this chapter on patents, I only write about domestic patents, those being registered in the United States and pertaining to the United States. International patents are a broader category involving many countries and conflicting laws that are way beyond my area of experience or the scope of this book.

Part 3 - Intellectual Property

There are a lot of books and other sources where you can find information related to international patents. Certainly you should consider consulting a patent attorney.

And by the way, at the start here, let me again give you my disclaimer: What I tell you about patents is my general point of view but it should not be seen as legal advice. If you have specific concerns or questions you should consult a patent attorney who can gave you the kind of specific legal advice you may need.

There are three categories of patents in the United States:

1. Plant patent

2. Design patent

3. Utility patent

A plant patent covers vegetables, fruits, and other plants that you might see in a field. The details about how you can actually get a patent on plants are beyond the scope of this book.

A design patent protects designers of products from unfair use of their design. Apple might choose to apply to get a patent on the design of the iPhone. General Motors might choose to apply to get a patent on the design of the Escalade truck. Nike, the sports shoe company, might seek a design patent on their shoe designs.

And then there's the utility patent. The utility patent is the kind of patent most people are referring to when they talk about a patent. The utility patent covers the functionality, the way the mechanisms work in a particular invention. Think of the "chip clip" that you place on an open bag of potato chips to reseal it after it has been opened.

Before the chip clip, people might have used an old clothes pin or other types of clasps for the same purpose, but now consumers commonly use chip clips. I don't know if it is patented or not, but if you were to try to patent it you might describe it as "a jaw-like device with a spring in it that connects the two sides. When you press the tabs on the ends of the two sides, the spring releases or stretches and allows you to place the jaws over a bag. When you release the pressure on the tabs, the jaws close, thereby sealing the contents of the bag inside the bag."

Chapter 14 - Patent

Of course, what I just gave you is the layperson's explanation of how a patent application might describe the invention. Obviously an acceptable description is more complex than that. That's why you have attorneys.

But keep in mind that people get patents on their devices to prohibit others from developing devices that function in the *same way* to solve the same problem or set of problems.

For instance, when you press the tabs on a chip clip, the jaws open and allow you to place the jaws over some other material. Release the tabs and the jaws close. What causes it to function that way is the spring and the depression of the tabs. Another inventor might circumvent that patent and engineer around it by using a rubber band instead of a spring and claiming they have a different invention.

So your claim has to be more inclusive in an attempt to cover not only the spring and the rubber band but any other restraining or tension devices you can think of as well. While you're trying to be as broad as possible, without infringing on what someone else's invention is already doing, the patent examiner is going to want you to be as specific as possible. So the application process can get very complex. Consult an attorney.

Most people, when they make reference to a patent, are thinking about a utility patent. What often precedes a utility patent application – or what's also called a regular patent application – is a provisional patent application.

Provisional Patent Application

The provisional patent application (PPA), by itself, will NOT result in a patent despite its name. It's simply an application that precedes or can precede a regular utility patent application.

A provisional patent application buys you one year of time to file the regular utility patent application. During that year, you can continue to develop your idea, make a prototype, if you have not already done so, and, more importantly, test the waters of the marketplace to see if your idea can float commercially. You can do all of this before you spend the time, resources, and effort applying for a regular patent.

The PPA is actually a placeholder. It gives you a priority date ahead of your actual regular application. For instance, if you file a provisional patent application on September 1, 2020, that date will be viewed as your regular patent application filing date provided you file it before September 1, 2021.

Part 3 - Intellectual Property

If someone comes after September 1, 2020, and files a regular patent application for the same invention, your application date will precede theirs as soon as you formally file the regular application.

The cost to file a PPA is relatively inexpensive depending on your income and whether you are a large or small business. Depending on certain parameters it could be as little as $65.

But typically the filing fee will be somewhere around $100 or $120. On top of that, you'll have legal fees if you hire an attorney to fill out the application for you and make any necessary drawings. An attorney will charge you anywhere from $500 to $1,500. If it gets over $1,500, either you have a complex invention or you have an expensive attorney.

Or, you can file the provisional application yourself. Some inventors' consultants, including myself, recommend that the average independent inventor file the provisional themselves because it's not that difficult, particularly if you have any background in engineering or it helps if you are an artist and can draw a detailed picture of the invention and its components. While neither is necessary to file, these talents or expertise can be helpful when filing a patent application of any kind.

Also, you can purchase software that will help you to actually prepare the provisional application. You can buy the software for less than $200. Go to my website, www.thesimpleplan.com for updated info or check out www.patentwizard.com

Whether you file the provisional application yourself or through an attorney, it's not that expensive, and it's usually a good first step on the road to filing for a regular patent.

Once you've filed the PPA, you can spend the next year completing the six steps of *The Simple Plan* and determining what's going on with the invention. However, during that time you still cannot make your invention public and you cannot expose it to the general public. If you make your invention public, in any way, you have one year and only one year to file a regular utility application. If you don't, you will lose your potential patent right forever.

If you have filed a PPA and have NOT made it public, you have the one year to use the PPA filing date. If you miss that deadline, you can still file a regular patent application. You just cannot use the PPA priority date.

Making your invention "public" includes, but is not limited to:

- making your invention available for sale on the Internet or at a swap meet
- exposing it to the public either in print or online through, for instance, a magazine article
- talking about it on social media
- displaying it on a website
- displaying it at a trade fair or conference; or
- any other way that lets a broader public know about the invention

Any one of these methods starts the clock ticking. You have one year to file a regular application after exposing it to the public. If you do not file a regular application within that time, you will lose your right to get a patent on that invention forever. So you must bear this in mind.

During the year from the time you file a PPA, or from the time you begin step 1 of *The Simple Plan*, to the time you file for a regular application, you will want to keep the invention confidential as much as possible. So, you should require everyone within your closed group of experts, friends and family and potential customers who review or test your invention, to sign a non-disclosure agreement, as we discussed in chapter 4. In addition to requiring them to keep your invention confidential, the NDA will provide a paper trail demonstrating that the idea was always kept confidential and not being made public.

Is a Patent Even Needed for Success?

Is a patent necessary? Do you need to have a patent in order to make money with your invention? Well, I don't know if the answer is obvious to you or not, but it is no! You do not need a patent to make money with your invention.

The problem is this: Many inventors *think* they need a utility patent in order to market their invention. Nothing could be further from the truth. In fact, a lot of companies are moving away from patents altogether because they can be expensive and time consuming.

Many inventions out there are not patented!

What is more critical to the success of any new product, in my view, is to be the first one to market with the invention. If you are the first to market, you can capture a large market share as well as brand recognition, both of which can be more valuable than the patent.

However, if you have a complex invention, one that has a lot of bells and whistles or a lot of moving parts, it involves new technology, or it is entrenched in technology, then, yes, you probably should get a patent. If your invention is so novel, so innovative, a patent might be helpful in delaying competition while you try to capture market share.

Should You Patent a Fad Item?

If you have an inexpensive idea and an inexpensive product, you probably don't need a patent, particularly if your invention is more of a fad. If it's only going to be in the marketplace for a short period of time, a couple of years or so, don't waste your money on a patent because it will be two to three years, maybe more, before the patent is issued. By then you either will have missed your window of opportunity to capture market share for the invention or, if you have already put it on the market, the invention will have already started to lose steam by the time the patent is issued.

The whole purpose of a patent is to prohibit others from using your technology, your mechanism, to solve the same problem. If your product is only going to be on the market for a short period of time, then you probably don't need to worry about prohibiting others. Instead, you need to concern yourself with being the *first to market* and gaining as much market share and brand recognition as possible for the short-lived item.

Just get it out there first! Make as much money as you can and move on after the product dies. Getting a patent won't be of much benefit to you if the product is already dead by the time the patent is issued.

Is a Patent "Protection"?

A patent allows you to monopolize the rights to use the patented utility in a product. No one else may, without your consent. And if they do, you can sue them, after they have already infringed on those rights.

But I laugh when people say, "I want patent *protection,*" or "How do I *protect* my idea from being infringed in the first place?"

You can't really protect your idea with a patent. People have this false

Chapter 14 - Patent

view that a patent will protect you like a suit of armor protects the wearer in battle.

But a patent *is not* a suit of armor! It doesn't defend you against infringement. What a patent does is gives you *offensive rights* to go after the infringer.

The government doesn't go after them for you; it's not their concern. It's your patent; you have to defend it, using the offensive rights that you have gained by receiving a patent.

So a patent is not a suit of armor. It's more like a sword that you wield as you go after the infringer in the patent battlefield of the courtroom.

What is required in this litigious society for you to go after an infringer? First, you have to file a patent infringement lawsuit.

You could spend hundreds of thousands if not millions of dollars going after a patent infringer and, even though you have a patent, the outcome of your lawsuit will *not* be certain. Yes, you read that right. *Even though you have a patent*, when you file a lawsuit against an apparent infringer, *it does not mean that you will win.*

And even if you win and the infringer is required to pay money damages, you may not actually receive any of the money damages awarded.

So, you could go after the infringer, win the battle against him, shut him down or prevent his company from infringing further on your invention, and still not get any money out of him. Or, of course, you could lose the litigation altogether!

Sometimes the defendant can poke holes in an issued patent. For instance, they can charge that you, the patent owner, exposed it publicly before you said you did and so you shouldn't have gotten a patent in the first place.

Or, they can charge that the concept or the mechanism that you claimed in your patent application was already claimed in a previous patent that the patent examiner missed, meaning that someone else had a patent that was no longer active and now the patented invention is in the public domain. Or, someone else has a patent on the same claim that you claimed and you are – even though you have a patent – infringing on someone else's patent.

The "infringer" can make all kinds of affirmative defensive claims, some of which they might even be able to prove. This means you could have a hard battle ahead of you. At worst, the patent could be invalidated; at best, you win the patent infringement claim but now you have to either go after the money that you won as a result of the lawsuit and/or shut them down, which may not even matter if your product is beginning to decline anyway because advanced technology has made it obsolete.

Let us suppose you get a patent that lasts you seventeen years from the date of issuance. Who cares if, after four or five years, the technology has surpassed it and no one cares about your product anymore, or your product no longer has market appeal because someone else has come up with a product that doesn't infringe on your patent, and that performs the same function more effectively and more efficiently. Your patent really means nothing now because the new product is going to beat you anyway and it doesn't infringe.

The Patent Decision

As you can see, obtaining a patent can be a sound business decision. But it's not the be-all and end-all. You, as the independent inventor, have to decide whether you want to spend $15,000 or more in three years trying to get a patent that:

- is no guarantee against infringement; and
- requires you to spend an unknown amount of money suing to enforce your rights with an uncertain outcome.

Or a patent on an invention that either:

- has a short life span;
- may not be commercially successful; or
- may be obsolete in a few years.

The above are all points you must consider.

So, do you really need to get a patent?

Well, as I said previously, if I invented a simple product with a *short life span,* I wouldn't personally worry about getting a patent. I'd just try to use the money that I would spend on a patent to try to get my product out there as quickly and as effectively as possible.

However, if you have a high-tech product, like a Dyson vacuum cleaner, and you created new vacuum cleaner technology, then, yes, you probably want to go ahead and get a patent. If you are Apple and you create a whole new smartphone technology, yes, you probably want to get a patent.

You Can't Patent an Idea

You can't patent an idea. We saw earlier how the chip clip solved the problem of how to keep contents of a bag fresh after the package has been opened. You can patent the functionality of the chip clip. You can patent how it is designed and the mechanisms involved in its functionality. But, you can't patent the idea of *sealing* a potato chip bag.

A patent doesn't prevent someone else from *solving that same problem of sealing a potato chip bag in a different way,* such as with a new kind of zipper, and getting a patent on the new way, the zipper.

The competing inventor then comes up with new bags that have the zipper lock at the top that solves the same problem your chip clip solves. If, in the view of the consumer, the zipper lock solves the problem more effectively, more efficiently, and maybe even more inexpensively than your chip clip, it will eat into your market share if it doesn't destroy your invention commercially altogether.

The Problem with Patents

The problem with patents, in my view, is that they are not protection. They only give you offensive rights. If someone infringes on your patent, your solution is to sue, with no certainty of outcome. You never know how much money it is going to cost you from start to finish. And even if you win a financial claim and you win financial damage, it doesn't mean you're going to be able to collect.

Mattel and a company called MGA have been in litigation since 2005. MGA made a line of dolls called Bratz, which Mattel thought they didn't have the right to make. Initially Mattel won the lawsuit; then the other side appealed and won. Then Mattel appealed and the two sides went back and forth for years, both spending millions of dollars on an uncertain outcome. As of this writing, they are still fighting. The only winners are the companies' patent attorneys.

One minute you win; the next minute you lose. You just never know. I'm not saying all this to scare you. I'm just trying to help you see the reality of dealing with a patent and filing claims and deciding whether or not it's really protection. Unless you have a stomach for litigation and for spending a lot of money, don't think a patent is going to protect you or be there to stop your infringers.

You have to make an effort to stop infringers. The patent is a tool you use to say, "Hey, there, you can't make that because it infringes on my patent." You want the infringing company to be shut down. You want it to stop producing the infringing product.

To make this happen, you have to present your argument to a judge or a jury and convince them not only that the patent is valid but also that the infringer is indeed infringing on your patent. All the while, the infringing side will be trying to prove that their product doesn't infringe. Meanwhile, you're spending a lot of money. So think about all of that.

And think also about the possibility that technology will make your patent obsolete in the near future, so it won't matter that you have a patent.

Conclusion

I've raised a lot of arguments that may make you think that you should not apply for a patent. That is not my goal here. What I'm saying is, be careful. Look at what you've got. If you've got a product with a short life span, really contemplate whether you should spend the money seeking a patent because the product will likely be obsolete by the time the patent is issued and all of that time and money will have been wasted.

If you have a product that has a long life span and is somewhat complex, and is truly unique and novel, new technology that is going to be expensive to build and to test, *then, yes, get a patent.* Spend the money because obviously you will want to try to hold off anyone else from infringing on it.

It doesn't mean they won't. However, at least sometimes a patent will scare off companies because they will know that, if they lose a patent infringement suit and all the stars are not lined up properly for them, they could lose a lot of money and be shut down.

So these are factors to consider when you're looking at a patent. I hope this information helps you to decide whether or not seeking a patent is right for you and your invention.

Chapter 14 - Patent

If you decide that it is right and you make the decision to go for a patent, I recommend that you file a provisional patent application first. It is less expensive than a regular utility patent application and it buys you time to further investigate the potential of your invention before submitting a regular utility patent application. You may even be able to secure a license deal with the PPA as your IP.

Chapter 15

Copyright

"Enthusiasm: A little thing that makes a BIG difference."
Unknown

"Pursue one great decisive aim with force and determination."
Carl von Clausewitz

Copyright, like a patent, is an offensive right that enables you to go after someone who infringes on it. Copyright covers the visual or auditory expression of your ideas. For games, it covers the instructions. Other examples of creations covered by copyright include:

- song lyrics

- music

- art

- movies

- books

- graphics

- sculptures

Unlike a patent, which provides seventeen years of exclusive rights, a copyright lasts the lifetime of the author plus seventy years. That's great! Your heirs can benefit from your copyrights many years after you're gone. I truly appreciate this fact about the copyright laws. They give creators a strong, long-term benefit.

Copyright Termination Provision

Copyrights also provide another advantage. There are laws that allow you, after you've issued a license of your copyright, to terminate the license if you wish.

199

Part 3 - Intellectual Property

Let's look at an example of this. Let's say you wrote the book called *My New Book*. When you licensed that book to your publisher, you may have only gotten a thousand bucks because you didn't know it was going to be a big hit.

Well, the beauty of a copyright is that there are laws in place that allow you to end the license after a set period of time, thereby giving you the chance to benefit from your now "hit" copyrighted work. They're called "copyright termination laws." This set of laws allows you to terminate any license deal you have made at the end of thirty-five years. If you live long enough, you can terminate it every thirty-five years as the author. You could terminate a license and get a new licensee, or reissue a license to the current licensee.

The law, the Copyright Act of 1976, was instituted to allow people who have given up their copyrights or licensed them to other people or entities to get another bite of the apple.

It's a very interesting law. Again, consult a copyright attorney who can help you to understand it, if, in fact, you are considering a copyright. It's good to know the intricacies of this law so that, as you are interested in licensing your copyright, you can weave your license agreement in a way that makes it even easier for you to use the termination laws to terminate that deal in thirty-five years.

By the way, your heirs can also terminate, even if you're gone, if they can get a better deal in the future. However, your heirs can only terminate once, whereas you as the author can terminate every thirty-five years as long as you are alive.

Anyway, talk to an attorney for more detail about this if you choose. By the way, as with the other portions of this book, you need to consult an IP attorney on any issues or questions you have personally in your specific situation. This is my disclaimer. I'm not offering legal advice here. I'm just giving you some general information and my understanding of how I view copyrights, patents, and trademarks based on my experiences.

Copyright's Offensive Rights

Copyright covers the visual or audio expression of your ideas. Examples are printed material, recorded material, ideas published on the Internet, and sculptures. It will "protect" you from infringers in the way that patents protect you against infringers, by giving you offensive rights.

200

Chapter 15 - Copyright

If someone were to breech my copyright, for instance, the government doesn't go after the infringer for me. I have to go after them. That means I have to spend money through legal counsel, an expensive undertaking that would require me to be up to that sort of challenge.

Typically, infringement does not happen that often. As we talked about earlier, when it comes to inventor paranoia, proven products might be stolen but ideas generally are not.

Counterfeiting

Once you create a product that's a hit, that has a great market, and people are buying it like hotcakes, then you have to be concerned that someone may try to knock it off or steal it outright. If they do, and if you have properly registered your copyright, you actually may receive help from the government (in counterfeiting situations), which will view the theft as a criminal act.

Some copyright owners faced a big problem when other companies were counterfeiting their works and importing them from various parts of the world into this country, claiming or trying to sell them as though they were produced by the original publishers or producers. In cases like these the government would seize these shipments and file criminal charges for counterfeiting, and so forth.

A counterfeit is an imitation, usually one that is made with the intent of fraudulently passing it off as genuine. Counterfeit products are often produced with the intent to take advantage of the established worth and brand of the imitated product.

Products that often face counterfeiting include CD's and DVD's, music, movies, software, and fine art.

However, generally speaking, if a person infringes on your copyright by producing a product that contains elements of your product the same way as yours, but they don't represent it as your product and they call it something else, and they have other utility related to it, then that *may be* more of an infringement issue than a government criminal issue related to counterfeiting. Again, you need to talk to your attorneys about these types of matters.

Part 3 - Intellectual Property

Filing a Copyright Registration

You can easily file online at www.copyright.gov It costs less than $100 and you can do it yourself. You don't have to go through any major hurdles.

In fact, you actually have a copyright the minute you put your ideas in a concrete form, such as print, video, recording, or Internet. But, to be able to sue in court, you have to register it with the government.

When I wrote the initial instructions for Phase 10, Dice Baseball, TimeSpan, WordMaster, and the other games I've invented, I immediately owned the copyright.

I could have, and did, put a copyright symbol © on those printed instructions and was perfectly legal. In fact, that's what you're asked to do by the government when you have a copyright regardless of its registration status. You don't have to but it's a good idea because it serves notice that you have a copyright.

However, you may still want to register with the government. You do this by filling out a form on the U.S. Copyright Office's website I've cited above. It's just a page or two. You send that in to the government along with three samples of the work that you're trying to register. It takes them a few months to send you the document that demonstrates that it is in fact registered.

Conclusion

Again, consult your attorney if you have an issue in regard to your copyright. As you have seen, copyrights are valuable to have, inexpensive to obtain, and long lasting. It is very easy to apply for a registered copyright. In order to sue for infringement your copyright must be registered.

Chapter 16

Trademark

"Goals without time limits are only wishes."
Unknown

"The future belongs to those who believe in the beauty of their dreams."
Eleanor Roosevelt

A trademark is a word or design that identifies a particular company's brand or product. The trademarked expression or design may not be used by any other company without permission of the trademark holder. Examples of trademarks include company logos, company symbols, product names and symbols, and company names and/or symbols.

In this chapter, we are going to discuss primarily how a trademark relates to the name of your new consumer product invention.

For example, I have a registered trademark for the name Phase 10. The names of my other games are trademarked as well: TimeSpan, Stake Your Stash, and most of the others games I've invented. Other games by Mattel, my licensee, are also trademarked, including Uno, Apples to Apples, and Monopoly.

People who know Phase 10 recognize the brand. So, I have created spinoffs of the original Phase 10 card game that utilize the same brand name – Phase 10:

- Phase 10 Masters Edition
- Phase 10 Twist
- Phase 10 Dice
- Phase 10 Kids
- Phase 10 MOD

This is called "brand extension." All of these brand extensions use the

Phase 10 brand because it is recognizable to people who love the game and excites them to buy the spinoffs.

Other brand owners do the same. The Coca-Cola brand is recognizable all over the world. When you see that brand, you expect a certain quality and taste to that soft drink. If you go to McDonald's, home of the trademarked golden arches, and you order a Big Mac, also trademarked, you expect a certain quality and taste. Apple's symbol trademark is an apple with a bite taken out of it. All these are symbols of products and companies. Customer expectations are based on these brands.

Your goal is to develop a strong recognizable brand around your product. You develop this brand in part with a strong trademark. A trademark might be considered "strong" if it clearly distinguishes itself from others. This is especially important to consumer products. No manufacturer wants their product to be confused with that of their competition.

So I recommend that you get a trademark on your consumer product. If it's going to be sold at retail to a consumer, a trademark adds value to product and can later, after the first product is successful, serve as a brand for future products.

Life of a Trademark

A trademark has to be maintained every ten years, which means you are required to send in a fee to the government every ten years that says to them, "Hey, we are still actively using the trademark." The costs of maintenance are detailed on the USPTO.gov website.

However, if you continue to use the trademark and pay the maintenance fee, your trademark can last forever. Compare that to the limited lives of the patent and the copyright that we discussed in the last two chapters.

So a trademark is vital to differentiating your product now and its long-term future.

How to Register Your Trademark

Registering a trademark is simple. I've done it myself. The form that you have to fill out is just a page or two. You can do it online at the USPTO. gov website. It costs $400 or less depending on how you file.

Of course, you can hire a patent attorney to do it for you. In that case you will have to add the cost of an attorney's legal fee.

Chapter 16 - Trademark

Trademark Search

No search is required to file a patent or register a copyright. Of course, without conducting a search before filing a patent, you spend your money to file facing a higher risk of rejection because of prior art or running into a previously filed patent. I highly recommend you conduct a trademark search before filing for a trademark registration.

The government has a website that allows you to do the search easily yourself or your trademark attorney can do it for you. You can search trademarks using the same site noted above. The search is based on keywords of the name you seek to trademark.

A search is necessary to make certain that your trademark is not infringing on someone else's trademark. You're going to spend most of your money on this critical step. In fact, it will likely be the most expensive step in the trademark registration process.

The cost of a thorough trademark search, if you hire an attorney, is maybe a thousand bucks or so, depending on who does it and their reputation. In any case, the cost is not prohibitive and it is a lot less expensive than the cost to defend yourself in court if you are accused of violating someone else's trademark.

Once you have conducted the search, and if you are confident the trademark you want is available, then you should proceed with filing for the trademark, as I described above.

Like the patent and the copyright, registering the trademark does not defend you against infringement of the trademark; it gives you offensive rights to go after someone who you believe has already infringed on your trademark.

Getting ownership of a trademark is definitely worth the money and the effort.

Trademark Can Build a Brand Legacy

Phase 10 is a legacy for me. It's a brand that I hope will last my lifetime and that of my heirs. This should be your goal as well, to develop a product and brand that will continue to provide income for a long time.

Furthermore, with a strong brand you can develop other products that are extensions of the original and use the credibility that is already attached to your brand name through your first product to more quickly build credibility for your succeeding products. You can even spin off into other areas of revenue while building upon the same brand.

Licensing Your Trademark

If someday you license your invention and the trademark associated with it, you must be careful to make sure you maintain or oversee the quality of the product. This is important because the brand will stand for the quality associated with it, whether it's good quality or bad. The consumer will come to expect the same quality, taste, function, colors, and other traits associated with the brand.

So if you have a licensee, you have to make sure you are receiving samples annually, at least, from them, so that you can check and maintain the quality associated with your brand.

If you don't continue to oversee the quality by receiving samples of the product, there are provisions in trademark law that may cause you to lose your trademark rights. Once that happens, any agreement that you, the licensor, sign with a licensee will be considered a "naked license." If you have granted a "naked license" you could lose your trademark right. So again, consult your trademark attorney who can give you more details about "naked license" and how to avoid this in your license agreement with your licensee.

Also, make sure your license agreement details which party, you or the licensee, is responsible for maintaining the trademark registration and who will pay for it. In addition, the agreement should further detail who will apply for, own, and maintain any trademarks registered in foreign countries.

Conclusion

A trademark is important to have. I highly recommend that you register your name, your logo, and any defining symbols of your company or your product. If you have a consumer product, you definitely want to brand it. Branding starts by getting a trademark. Very, very important.

* * *

Summary of All IP Rights: Patent, Copyright, Trademark

In the last three chapters, I've given you some good ideas concerning "protection" of your invention. More importantly, I've given you some good ideas on how to grow your invention by branding it, getting a patent when it is advisable, and avoiding a patent where it's not advisable or necessary. I've also encouraged using a copyright and/or trademark to your advantage where appropriate to build a legacy and maintain your offensive rights.

That's what patents, copyrights, and trademarks can do, provide you with offensive rights. So do other forms of offensive rights, such as "trade secrets." If you are interested in learning more about those other forms of "protection," consult your IP attorney.

There are several good books out there on these subjects that will help you to understand and appreciate how you can best maintain your intellectual property rights. I list some of them on my website: www.thesimpleplan.com

Holding onto your intellectual property rights with a patent or PPA, a copyright, or a trademark makes it easier for you to get a license agreement because it gives you perceived ownership of your invention. Maintaining that perception is more difficult if you don't have some form of IP ownership.

But if you do have a registered IP, a licensee will look at your intellectual property as though it is an actual something that they are buying or licensing and that you actually own. Whether those rights have been issued or are still pending doesn't matter, which is why I recommend filing a PPA as the first step in the patent process.

Also, by owning IP, you discourage most would-be-infringers from infringing on your rights. Many will not want to go through the time and expense of developing an infringing product only to face litigation, the possible shutdown of their business, expense of a lawsuit, and costs of a large financial award to you.

Without any intellectual property rights, some prospective licensees will even question your ownership of your invention.

AFTERWORD

Well, that's it. I've just outlined the simple steps, six of them, you should follow to make millions from your ideas. While each step requires some work, you can and should complete them in the order prescribed, with the possible exception of step 4.

Step 4, filing the PPA, is the only "floating" step. If you want to *eventually file a patent application* for a regular, plant, or design patent and you need to build a complex and costly prototype, you should file the PPA before you build it in step 2. Or, if you need to test your prototype with a wide audience of potential users, advisors, industry experts, and others and you wish to go beyond an NDA, you may consider filing a PPA before step 3, the product evaluation.

For most of you, however, use a non-disclosure agreement when testing your prototype and talking to others about your invention. Only consider filing a PPA and eventual patent application when it makes sense to do so. Remember, a patent only gives you offensive rights; you must spend money to enforce those rights. For most of you, your invention will not justify the expense of the patenting process.

Further, a patent is not a prerequisite to making money from your invention. The only prerequisite is a truly marketable invention.

I may have been a little hard on securing patents. I may sound like I'm totally against them. Well, I'm not. I just want you to discover the real potential of your invention before embarking on the patenting process. So much money is wasted each year by inventors seeking patents on ideas that are NOT commercially viable. So pursue a patent for your invention with caution.

The most important step of *The Simple Plan* is the first, the market evaluation. Definitely perform this vital first step, first! The results will inform you as to whether or not your invention has real commercial potential. If you put any of the other steps ahead of this one, you are likely setting yourself up for failure and a loss of money.

Afterword

The goal of this book was not to give you every detail of every step in the inventing process. For instance, I could write multi-hundred-page books each on the details of patents, copyright, trademarks, and licensing. Whole libraries are devoted exclusively to each of these subjects.

Rather, my purpose was to inform you of the straightforward steps necessary for successful inventing. I've supplied enough detail for that purpose. My goal was to keep it simple, to break down the process to the truly necessary steps, and to outline the best order and approach to fulfilling those steps.

You can go to my website for updated information and more details on various topics related to inventing. I also write a blog covering everything related to the inventing process and entrepreneurship.

Visit http://www.thesimpleplan.com

As you travel along the road toward your goal of inventing success, you will face obstacles. Some will come from the world around you while others will emerge from within you.

The external obstacles usually are easily identified. You will see them and, hopefully, you will be able to overcome them. One such obstacle – those people who will try to discourage you needlessly. They will not see the potential of your ideas and, therefore, will think you are wasting your time and money. While it is important to take objective criticism of your invention, make sure the source has knowledge of what they speak.

Other external obstacles will be financial. Sources for the money you will need to bring your invention to market may not be apparent. Make sure you seek out the potential resources of those around you to help you in your efforts. Friends and family, those who believe in what you are doing, will be your first line of financial help along the way.

Most external obstacles can be overcome with creativity and imagination. Use your imagination, the same imagination you used to create your inventive ideas, to figure out ways to overcome the obstacles you will most surely face.

The most problematic obstacles you will face, however, are the internal ones, those "negative mindsets" I referred to in chapter 6 that come from inside you and can be the most damaging and hard to overcome. You could be your own invention's greatest obstacle! So by all means, avoid these negative tendencies and increase your chances of success.

Finally, work hard! TAKE ACTION! Make it your goal to accomplish something everyday that will move you closer to your goal of getting your invention on the market. Every little step you take will move you in the right direction. After all, "How can a man eat an elephant? One bite at a time."

Follow the steps of *The Simple Plan*. By doing so you will greatly improve your chance of success.

I wish you happy and successful inventing!

About the Author

Ken Johnson was 12-years old when he created his first invention, a board game he called Dice Baseball, with the help of his brother Keith and sister Phyllis.

At 19, Ken started a game publishing company in the basement of his parents' inner-city Detroit home. There he manufactured and sold his games nationwide to the then-largest retailer in the United States, KMart.

Ken's most successful game is Phase 10, first published in 1982. Today, Phase 10 is the second-best-selling card game of all time, behind only Uno. It is sold in over 25 countries around the world.

Since 2013, Ken his been a sought-after speaker to groups of inventors and entrepreneurs all over the United States. He has personally consulted hundreds of inventors and helped many to obtain royalty-producing licenses for their inventions

Ken currently owns several businesses and is an active member of various boards dedicated to inventing, entrepreneurship, and the academic achievement of students in grades K-12. He sits on the board of trustees of Spring Arbor University.

The Simple Plan is a distillation of Ken's many years of experience as both an inventor and an entrepreneur producing and selling his invented products.

Ken can be heard on his podcast: Successful Inventing – available on Apple, Google, Spotify, and other popular podcast platforms.

You can reach Ken at kenjohn1@att.net.

Visit Ken's website at: www.kenjohnsonspeaks.com

Contact Ken directly for speaking engagements!

Contact him also for bulk book sale pricing.

Your honest review on Amazon is greatly appreciated.

Be well and safe!

Made in United States
North Haven, CT
06 January 2023

30664925R00138